# THE *ALABAMA* AFFAIR

## The British Shipyards Conspiracy in The American Civil War

David Hollett

An  Publication

**Published by:-**


Avid Publications,
Garth Boulevard
Bebington,
Wirral,
Merseyside.UK
CH63 5LS
Telephone / Fax: (44) 0151  645  2047


e-mail info @ AvidPublications.co.uk

website  http//www.AvidPublications.co.uk

**OTHER BOOKS AND VIDEOS  ARE AVAILABLE DIRECT FROM AVID PUBLICATIONS, DETAILS OF THESE ARE AT THE REAR OF THIS BOOK**

**THE ALABAMA AFFAIR**

- The British Shipyards Conspiracy in The American Civil War
**by DAVID HOLLETT**

ISBN 1 902964 32  2  © David Hollett 1993

FIRST PRINTED 1993
THIS EDITION 2002
A CIP record for this book is available from the British Library

# Preface

The winter of 1860-61 was a momentous one in the history of the United States of America. Abraham Lincoln had just been elected President, but this was soon followed by the secession of South Carolina from the Union. Events rapidly came to a crisis: soon Mississippi, Florida, Louisiana, Alabama, Georgia and Texas joined the rebellion. These states gathered together and called themselves the Confederate States of America. Jefferson Davis was elected President, and within weeks shots were exchanged. The long and bloody American Civil War had begun. The North was waging a war for its national life.

Freedom and slavery were the issues underlying the struggle. Jefferson Davis and the plantation owners of the 'Deep South' saw the enslaved negro plantation workers as a 'species of property'; and they demanded the 'right' to take this 'property' with them into the new territories, a concept enshrined under Article 1V, Section 2 of the Confederate Constitution:

"In all such territory, the institution of negro slavery, as it now exists in the Confederate States, shall be recognised and protected by Congress and by the territorial government; and the inhabitants of the several Confederate States and Territories shall have the right to take to such Territory any slaves lawfully held by them in any of the States or Territories of the Confederate States."

Lincoln, who was born in Kentucky on 12 February 1809, was the son of an illiterate pioneer farmer and, like the slaves of the South, was no stranger to hard manual toil. However, he took the opposite view to the powerful plantation owners, encapsulating the political situation in his immortal words:

"The house divided against itself cannot stand. I believe this Government cannot endure permanently half slave and half free. I do not expect it will cease to be divided. It will become all one thing or all the other. Either the opponents of slavery will arrest the further spread of it and place it where the public mind shall rest, in the belief that it is in the course of ultimate extinction; or its advocates will push it forward, till it shall become alike lawful in all the States, old as well as new, North as well as South."

From the outset the odds were stacked against the South. The North had a combined population of 22 million, while the seceding states had only 9 million; and 3 million of the latter were slaves, many of whom would soon be fighting for the North to gain their liberation. The North was highly industrialised, with a great many factories, foundries, mines, machine shops and shipyards manned by thousands of skilled, free workers. Significantly, the North also had a well developed merchant marine, trading to all parts of the world.

In stark contrast to this, the South was held in a social and economic 'time warp', being almost entirely dependent economically on one cash crop – slave-produced cotton. Almost all the South's requirements had to be obtained from abroad in exchange for this one commodity. Lincoln, well aware of this weakness, soon placed a blockade on the ports of the South, thus dealing the Confederates a vital blow.

The South responded by taking steps to build up its own naval strength by obtaining ships in Europe. The Confederate agent, Captain James Dunwoody Bulloch, was promptly sent to Liverpool, the port through which most slave-produced American cotton was imported, *en route* to the mills of Lancashire. Here there was much – though not universal – sympathy for the Confederate cause in business and shipping circles, motivated by a desire not to see cotton supplies or shipping disrupted.

In Liverpool, Bulloch acted as Chief Agent of the Confederate States Navy Department in Great Britain. His mission was to acquire 'commerce raiders' – ships capable of attacking and sinking Federal merchant shipping. He also encouraged the building of fast 'blockade runners' – small, fast steamers that would be able to dash through the line of United States ships blockading the South.

The first commerce raider he obtained on Merseyside was the *Florida*, built by Miller & Company, with engines by Fawcett & Preston. However, it was while he was negotiating this deal that he first went with a friend to the Birkenhead Ironworks, and was introduced to John Laird and his sons. It is more than likely that Bulloch had already heard of the Laird family, for some years previously they had built a river steamer for a Mr Lamar, a Savannah ship-owner, banker and cotton merchant. This vessel, named the *John Randolph*, with engines by Fawcett & Preston, had done sterling work for her owner, carrying thousands of tons of cotton down the Savannah river.

After detailed negotiations Bulloch placed an order with Laird & Company for a ship, yard number 290, which would soon be sailing under her true colours as the infamous raider *Alabama*. This ship, with other British-built Confederate raiders, was to do enormous damage to Federal shipping which, years after the conclusion of the war, was to cost the British Government £3,299,166 in compensation payments, through what became known as the 'Alabama Claims'. The whole issue placed a great strain on Anglo-American relations, nearly bringing the two nations to war at one stage. Although Laird & Company are well known for having built the *Alabama* and the 'Laird Rams' – *El Monassir* and *El Tousson* – for the Confederates, their contribution to the cause of the South as shipbuilders was far greater than this, for they also built seven blockade runners, two of which, together with the supply ship *Georgiana*, were actually owned by John Laird junior! Other Merseyside shipbuilders who contributed to the cause of the South by building vessels were Messrs Jones, Quiggin & Company of Liverpool, who built 16 blockade runners; Miller & Company who, apart from building the *Florida*, built six runners; Bowdler, Chaffer & Company who built a further three; and W.H. Potter & Sons who built the runners *Deer* and *Dream*.

When James Dunwoody Bulloch arrived in Liverpool, he was aware that the regime he served had just made the biggest blunder of the war. They had an option on ten first class Indiamen, but failed to complete the deal. Had this fleet been acquired, it would undoubtedly have swept the American coast from the Capes of the Chesapeake in the north to the Rio Grande in the south, breaking the Federal blockade. Bulloch worked diligently over the next few years to make up for this failure on the part of the Confederate leadership but, perhaps fortunately, not all his ventures were crowned with success.

For the Laird family the situation was ironic, for Macgregor Laird, younger brother of John Laird, had spent his entire adult life opposing the institution of slavery. However, Macgregor died on 27 January 1861, just before his family became involved with Bulloch and the Confederacy. One wonders if this involvement would have occurred had Macgregor Laird lived for a few more years. Soon after Macgregor died, John Laird gave active control of the shipyard to his sons William and John – chiefly because he had decided to stand for Parliament, and was in fact soon to become Birkenhead's first representative at Westminster.

In the House, John Laird spoke almost exclusively on matters relating to shipping, an industry in which he had a large vested interest. Back in Birkenhead he did much to develop the town. He remained active in local and national affairs until he died in October, 1874. The Laird shipyard, which John Laird did so much to develop, gained fame throughout the world for the construction of fine ships, but in America the name of John Laird will always be linked with the construction of the *Alabama*, and the Confederate cause she was built to serve.

The *Alabama* was eventually sunk by the United States ship *Kearsage*, which was commanded by Captain John Ancrum Winslow, a devoted Christian and outspoken opponent of slavery. Amongst the crew of the *Kearsage* were negro gunners who fought heroically to sink the notorious raider, each one of them fully aware that this vessel had been operating for too long in the interests of their oppressors.

This work covers the history of these Confederate vessels, the men who built them, and the Federal ships sent out to destroy them, against the perspective of contemporary military and political developments on both sides of the Atlantic. The concluding chapter also covers the immediate post-Civil War period, the assassination of Abraham Lincoln, and the reaction to this crime in Liverpool, where thousands of those who had been sympathetic to Abraham Lincoln and the cause of the North attended mass meetings to express their sorrow. Mention is also made of the infamous Ku Klux Klan, the sinister organisation established by defeated Confederate soldiers, and still active in America – a grim legacy of the Confederate rebellion of 1861 which still remains with us at the close of the twentieth century.

*David Hollett*

**ACKNOWLEDGEMENTS**

The author wishes to thank:-

The Department of Leisure Services and Tourism, Metropolitan Borough of Wirral;

Mr Colin Simpson and Mr. Phillip Eastwood of the Williamson Art Gallery and Museum, Birkenhead;

Carol Bidston, Mavis Beckerleg, and staff at Birkenhead Central Library for their help and co-operation.

My wife Vera, who gave much help and assistance whilst I was producing this book.

Front cover painting: from an original 'The Alabama' (Courtesy Williamson Art Gallery & Museum, Birkenhead)

# CONTENTS

Talk not of the property of the planter in his slaves. I deny the right; I acknowledge not the property. The principle, the feelings of our common nature rise in rebellion against it. Be the appeal made to the understanding or to the heart, the sentence is the same that rejects it. In vain you tell me of laws that sanction such a claim. There is a law above all the enactments of human codes - the same throughout the world - the same at all time .... It is the law written by the finger of God on the heart of man; and by that law, unchangeable and eternal, while men despise fraud and hate rapine and abhor blood, they will reject with indignation the wild and guilty phantasy that man can hold property in man.?

*Lord Henry Peter Brougham & Vaux*

**BY THE SAME AUTHOR**

| | |
|---|---|
| *From Cumberland to Cape Horn.* | **Fairplay Publications, London, 1984** |
| *Fast Passage to Australia* | **Fairplay Publications, London, 1986** |
| *Merseyside and the 19th Century Emigrant Trade to Australia.* | **Wirral Metropolitan Borough Council, 1987** |
| *Men of Iron-The Story of Cammell Laird Shipbuilders 1828 - 1991* | **Wirral Metropolitan Borough Council, 1992** |
| *The Conquest of the Niger by Land & Sea* | **Heaton Publishing, Abergavenny, April, 1995** |
| *Passage to the New World* | **Heaton Publishing, Abergavenny, May, 1995** |
| *Passage from India to El Dorado* | **Associated University Presses, Cranbury, New Jersey, USA, 1999** |
| *The Clwydian Way Long Distance Trail* | **Ist Edition: The Ramblers' Association, 2000** |
| | **2nd Edition: The Ramblers' Association, 2002** |

# CHAPTER 1

## EARLY DAYS IN THE CIVIL WAR

### A divided nation

On 4 March 1861 Abraham Lincoln was sworn in as President of the United States, a nation already divided by the secession of seven Southern states. As he stood on the east portico of the capitol he sought to reassure the nation of survival, saying, "The union of these states is perpetual...No state upon its own mere notion can get out of the union." While he spoke, soldiers with fixed bayonets stood guard, wary of assassination attempts. Though firmly opposed to slavery himself, Lincoln was acutely aware that not all of his potential supporters for the defence of the Union were so high-minded on the question of slavery. Accordingly, he made his public utterances on this controversial issue very carefully, presenting the war as one mainly in defence of the Union, rather than with the elimination of slavery as its main objective.

However, although flexible and careful on most matters, Lincoln was unambiguous in his outspoken opposition to the extension of slavery into the new territories. The son of illiterate settlers, his birthplace had been a crude log-cabin, perhaps not too dissimilar to the dwellings occupied by the enslaved negro plantation workers of the South. Like the Southern slaves he was also no stranger to hard manual labour, having spent his early days splitting fence rails, planting corn, and generally assisting the family in the hard life of early settler farmers. No doubt all of this influenced his attitude to the poor, oppressed and enslaved, shaping his philosophy and political position on the crucial issues of the day.

A totally different life-style was to shape the mind of young Jefferson Davis. Born in 1808, his family had moved south to Mississippi when he was very young. They found their anchorage in a small plantation near Woodville, Wilkinson County. Here his elder brother Joseph soon became the active head of the family and the patron of his younger brother Jefferson, many years his

*Early residence of Abraham Lincoln*

*Early residence of Jefferson Davis*

junior. Eventually Joseph Davis was considered one of the wealthiest men of the South, where wealth was based on one thing – slavery. It was this life of elitist plantation owners, not that of humble settlers, that was to influence the mind of young Jefferson Davis. To him, negro slaves were a species of property, which slave owners had a right to take into the new territories – the very issue on which Lincoln would not yield.(1)

Working with Davis was Alexander Stephens of Georgia, Vice President of the Confederacy. His infamous 'Cornerstone Speech', delivered at Savannah shortly after the establishment of the Confederacy, was his main political statement, and certainly the most revealing. Like many resolutions and declarations of the Confederates, it emphasised slavery as the fundamental cause of the war – and as the fundamental principle of the Confederacy:

"The new constitution has put at rest *forever* all the agitating questions relating to our peculiar institutions – African slavery as it exists among us – the proper *status* of the negro in our form of civilisation. *This was the immediate cause of the late rupture and present revolution.* Jefferson, in his forecast, had anticipated this, as the 'rock upon which the old Union would split'. He was right. What was conjecture with him, is now realized fact. But whether he fully comprehended the great truth upon which that rock stood, and stands, may be doubted. The prevailing ideas entertained by him and most of the leading statesmen at the time of the formation of the old Constitution were, that the enslavement of the African was in violation of the laws of nature; that it was wrong in principle, socially, morally and politically. It was an evil they knew not well how to deal with; but the general opinion of the men of that day was that, somehow or other, in the order of Providence, this institution would be evanescent and pass away. The idea though not incorporated in the Constitution, was the prevailing idea at the time. The Constitution, it is true, secured every essential guarantee to the institution while it should last, and hence no argument can be justly used against the constitutional guarantees thus secured, because of the common sentiment of the day.

*"Those ideas, however were fundamentally wrong. They were vested upon the assumption of the equality of the races. This was an error.* It was a sandy foundation, and the idea of a Government built upon it – when the 'storm came, and the wind blew, it fell'.

*"Our new Government is founded upon exactly the opposite ideas; its foundations are laid, its cornerstone rests, upon the great truth that the negro is not equal to the white man; that slavery, subordination to the superior race, is the natural and moral condition. This, our new Government, is the first in the history of the world, based upon this great physical, philosophical, and moral truth..."*.(2)

Armed with this brand of philosophical 'truth', Jefferson Davis and his deputy Stephens gathered their supporters around them. Soon the Confederate troops would be marching into battle, presenting themselves to the world as a legitimate 'rebel' government, struggling for their freedom and independence against the oppressive Lincoln administration of the United States. Their ability to speak of 'freedom', in the context of defending a regime constitutionally based on slavery, is hard to comprehend today.

## The siege of Fort Sumter

Meanwhile, events were moving towards their inevitable conclusion. When South Carolina had seceded, Major Robert Anderson, commanding the Federal forces in Charleston, secretly moved his garrison from Fort Moultrie to Fort Sumter. The question of whether his forces should be withdrawn or supported created something of a controversy in the closing weeks of the Buchanan administration and the opening weeks of Lincoln's. While the politicians of the North argued, the Confederacy moved quickly, taking over all but four of the forts, arsenals, and military posts in the South. Lincoln

*Planting the United States flag Fort Sumter. On surrender of the fort, Major Anderson offered his sword to General Beauregard, who returned it saying: "I am happy to return the sword of so brave an officer"*

Charleston harbour, on the orders of President Lincoln. Here he had shown true statesmanship, by informing Jefferson Davis that the Federal Government intended to supply Major Anderson and his men with food and water only, as this gave Davis two options – either to fire on the supply ship and thus precipitate war, or allow the ship to pass and lose face with the firebrands of South Carolina.

Davis responded by ordering General Beauregard to surround the fort with the 7,000 men under his command, asking for Anderson's surrender. He was then advised that Beauregard would give him one hour to change his mind, or the Confederate forces would open fire. It was 3.20am on 12 April. At 4.30am there was a thunderous roar, then a flash of light, as a huge mortar shell traced its thin red line through the early morning air. The first shot in the American Civil War had been fired – by the Confederates. Within

eventually decided to provision rather than reinforce the fort.

The drama now centred on Major Anderson and his ability to keep going with diminishing supplies. However, a supply ship was already on the way to the new island fort in minutes, hundreds of howitzers and mortars surrounding the fort were blazing, and the fort was surrounded by a vast ring of fire. Anderson stuck it out for two days, then surrendered. Amazingly there were no casualties, though not surprisingly Fort Sumter sustained a great deal of damage. Major Anderson and his men were allowed to leave on the Federal supply ship.

Soon after the reduction of Fort Sumter, the Virginia militia seized Harper's Ferry, an important military arsenal at the confluence of the rivers Shenandoah and Potomac, and the great naval arsenal and ship-building yards of Norfolk, where the James river discharges into Chesapeake Bay. Lincoln then issued a proclamation calling out 75,000 militia men. Davis responded with a counter-proclamation, inviting applications for letters of marque and reprisal to be granted under the Seal of the Confederate States against ships and property of the United States and her citizens.

In a further proclamation dated 19 April, Lincoln, after referring to the proposed letters of marque, declared that he had deemed it advisable to set on foot a blockade of the ports within the seven States in revolt, ''in pursuance of the laws of the United States and the law of the nations in such case provided''.(3)

The Federal Government now had the awesome task of patrolling 3,000 miles of coastline, with a navy of just 40 modern ships. The Confederates, on the other hand, were faced with the prospect of having their cotton exports stopped, and the importation of all they needed for war and peace terminated. The implications for the cotton and shipping interests in Liverpool, and the mill workers of Lancashire, were incalculable, but, paradoxically, it was the mill workers of Lancashire who were to side with Lincoln in the struggle, whereas those wealthy enough to weather the storm without undue suffering sided with the slave owners of the South.

## The early career of Raphael Semmes

The Confederates, fearing the effects of the blockade on their fragile economy, moved quickly, in a desperate effort to gain the upper hand. Within days of the fall of Fort Sumter, Commander Raphael Semmes, then acting as Chief of the Confederate States Light-house Bureau, contacted Mallory, Secretary of the Confederate States Naval Board at New Orleans, urging him to purchase the screw steamer *Habana* for conversion to a commerce raider. Mallory accepted the proposal, the ship was purchased, and the name promptly changed to *Sumter*. Perhaps rather to his surprise, Semmes was then ordered to assume command of the vessel, with the following men listed amongst his officers: Lieutenants John M. Kell, R.T. Chapman, John M. Stribling and William E. Evans – the surgeon being Francis L. Galt. As fate would have it, it was to be Semmes, with Kell acting as his 'Luff' or 1st Lieutenant, who were soon to enter the pages of history as Commander and 1st

Officer of the Laird-built commerce raider *Alabama*.(4)

Raphael Semmes, the leading light in this drama, was born in 1809, his parents being of French Catholic ancestry. Both his parents died while he was a young child, and the boy was brought up in Georgetown, DC, apparently in moderate circumstances, by an uncle. It was probably the influence of another uncle, Benedict J. Semmes, a Maryland planter and slave owner active in politics, which led to his appointment by President Adams as midshipman in the United States Navy, on 1 April 1826.

His active naval career began on 8 September 1826, when he reported for duty on a sloop-of-war of the Mediterranean Squadron. During a long probationary period he was to serve successively on the sloops *Lexington* and *Erie*, the frigate *Brandywine*, the schooner *Porpoise*, and the frigate *Constellation*, on the Mediterranean, West Indian, South American and Florida stations.

From 1837 to the outbreak of the Mexican war Semmes spent most of his time on survey duty on the southern coast and in the Gulf of Mexico on board the brig *Consort* and the steamer *Poinsett* (his first command), interspersed with tours ashore at the Norfolk and Pensicola navy yards. He was eventually detailed as flag-lieutenant to Commodore Connor; and he was onshore with the naval bombardment of Vera Cruz in March 1847.

During the period of peace, until 1861, he was on waiting-orders status more than half the time, during which time he practised

law. He was later to become Inspector of Clothing and Provisions at Pensicola, on sundry court-martial duty, then inspector of the 8th Light House District, before becoming a member of the Lighthouse Board. He became Commander on 14 September 1855. Philosophically committed to the cause of the Confederacy, Raphael Semmes resigned from the United States service on 15 February 1861, promptly making his way to the Confederate capital where he gave Congress his views on national defence. He was then sent to the North where he purchased munitions, ordnance machinery and ships. He made numerous contracts and succeeded in getting large quantities of percussion caps and powder shipped south before the outbreak of hostilities. During this long active absence he was appointed a commander from Alabama in the Confederate States navy. He returned from his mission in the North on 18 April, when he was relieved from his lighthouse duties. It was at this point in his long and interesting career that he was given command of the first commerce raider to operate under the flag of the Confederate States of America.(5)

When he received his new command the *Sumter* was still only the packet steamer *Habana* lying at her berth in New Orleans, and Semmes had to turn naval constructor and ordnance expert in order to get her rebuilt, equipped, and armed as a man-of-war. The ship that was to become the raider *Sumter* was a vessel of just 437 tons register, 184 feet long, 30 feet beam, 12 feet depth of hold, and rigged as a barquentine. To say that she was not ideally suited to her new role as a man-of-war would be something of an understatement, for she could only carry coal for eight days' steaming, and was slow under sail, as her propeller dragged.

For the next two months Semmes supervised the fitting out of the vessel, watching every detail as the battery was mounted, which consisted of an 8-inch gun pivoted amidships and four light 32 pounders in broadside. A crew of competent seamen was enlisted from the many merchant vessels trapped by the blockade at New Orleans, and on 3 June the ship was put in commission as a vessel of war of the Confederate States.(6) The orders given to Raphael Semmes were to "do the enemy's commerce the greatest injury in the shortest time".(7)

The *Sumter* put to sea on 30 June 1861, entering upon a game which was to require all the skill and experience that Semmes had aquired from his long and varied naval career. As well as being philosophically committed to his cause, there can be no doubt whatsoever that Semmes was a skilled mariner, well chosen for the role that he was about to play.

Meanwhile, the Federal Government had been active in moving ships to the South to implement the blockade. The *Niagara*, which had returned from Japan on 24 April, was sent to cruise off Charleston. The *Brooklyn* and *Powhatan* moved westward along the Gulf. Before 1 May, seven steamers of considerable size had been chartered in New York and Philadelphia. One of these, the *Keystone State*, chartered

by Lieutenant Woodhull and intended for use at Norfolk, was at her station in Hampton Roads just 48 hours after Woodhull had received his orders from Washington to secure a vessel. The *South Carolina* arrived off Pensacola on 4 June, and the *Massachusetts* was equally prompt in reaching Key West. Notwithstanding these efforts, the blockade can hardly be said to have been in existence until six weeks after it was declared by Lincoln, and then only at the principal ports.(8)

When Semmes took the *Sumter* to sea he chose Pass a' L'Outre for his exit from the Mississippi into the Gulf of Mexico, when the Federal sloop *Brooklyn* was a few miles off to overhaul a strange sail. The *Sumter* was well through the pass before she was detected by the *Brooklyn*, which immediately gave chase. The chase of the *Sumter* by the *Brooklyn* was a dramatic one – at one point Semmes was in such danger of being captured that he prepared to throw overboard his military chest and public papers. This trouble was soon averted, however, as with increased speed Semmes drew away from the Federal ship, the *Brooklyn* abandoning the pursuit about 4pm on 3 July.

While running along the coast of Cuba Semmes made the first of his many captures, the victim on this notable occasion being the barque *Golden Rocket*, of Maine. Her crew were taken off and the vessel burned. It was in this manner that Raphael Semmes began his long, and, in the opinion of many, over-active career, as a commanding officer in ships of the Confederate States Navy, or as the Federal government saw it, as a pirate and traitor – interpretations of his adventures afloat that the arrogant Semmes deeply resented!

## Bulloch in Liverpool

Whilst events were unfolding off the coast of America, another true son of the 'Deep South' was making his way to Liverpool. Captain James Dunwoody Bulloch, secret agent to the Confederate States of America, was a capable officer and well connected socially in America, having all the airs and graces of one brought up in 'Plantation Society' south of the Mason and Dixon Line.

Bulloch was born near Savannah in June 1823, his father, Major James Stephen Bulloch, being a member of the company under whose auspices the *Savannah* made her famous voyage across the Atlantic from Savannah to Liverpool. His half sister, Martha Bulloch, was destined to marry Theodore Roosevelt Senior, and was the mother of President Roosevelt. In 1839 James Bulloch became a midshipman in the United States navy. He served first on board the *United States* and later on the sailing sloop-of-war *Decatur*, on the Brazil station.

After service on the battleship *Delaware* he attended the navy school at Philadelphia in 1844-45. In 1849-51 he served in the coast survey. He then became active in the United States mail service as a naval commander, becoming identified with the shipping enterprises of New York. Immediately after the start of the Civil War he accepted, from Secretary Mallory, the foreign mission as agent of the Confederate navy to buy or build vessels in England.

Captain James Dunwoody Bulloch arrived in Liverpool on 4 June 1861. It was late in the day, and Bulloch was disappointed to find that most of the business houses were already closed, including the one he was primarily concerned with, Messrs Fraser, Trenholm & Company. He found lodgings for the night, and at an early hour next day made his way back to their premises to discuss his mission.(9)

The principal partner in this company was George Alfred Trenholm, who was subsequently to become Secretary of the Treasury of the Confederacy from July 1864 to April 1865. Trenholm was a tall handsome man, and fabulously wealthy; having made his money from the toil of plantation slaves, he now owned steamships, city business houses, hotels, wharves, stock in railroads and cotton presses. At the beginning of the Civil War Trenholm enjoyed almost unlimited credit in the United Kingdom, which convenient facility was used by Jefferson Davis and his Confederate Government, who had no credit with other nations, for the purchase of armaments, ships and supplies. Trenholm's company owned, or operated, a huge fleet of almost 60 ships, which brought in cargoes for the Confederates until the end of the war. Trenholm and his company were the authorised depository of Confederate funds abroad.

A year before the Civil War began, the associated firm of John Fraser & Company had proudly announced a line of sailing packets, with monthly schedules between Charleston and Liverpool. The Charleston *Daily Courier* also announced that the company were having an iron propeller ship built, capable of stowing 3,500 bales of cotton – exclusively for trade between Liverpool and Charleston. The company ships engaged in the packet line were the *Susan G. Owens*, *Eliza Bonsall*, *Gondar*, *Emily St Pierre*, and the *John Fraser*.

The house of Fraser, Trenholm & Company had established contact with John Laird, the shipbuilder of Birkenhead who would soon be working for the Confederacy, long before Bulloch arrived on the scene. They had discussed Charleston-Liverpool shipping ventures. Two months after South Carolina had seceded from the Union, on 22 February 1861, the people of Charleston had met to consider a proposal made by John Laird, and a Mr Wier. Their joint plan had been to establish a Liverpool and Charleston Steamship Company, a venture which would have required a capital outlay of some £150,000 to be raised in £10 shares, half in Charleston, the other half in Liverpool. John Laird and his sons were to build three substantial iron steamers of 1,800 tons, each powered by a 250 horse-power engine, at a cost of £47,000 for each vessel.(10) After a favourable report by a small committtee, a larger committee was formed to raise the substantial sums required. However, Laird's plan depended upon the establishment of the Confederacy without resort to war. One of the members of the small committee was W.L. Trenholm, of Fraser, Trenholm & Company.(11)

*The Fraser Trenholm Offices, 10 Rumford Place, Liverpool. (Chris Sarson)*

The involvement of Fraser, Trenholm with the Confederacy, and their links with the agent James Dunwoody Bulloch, were crucial to the cause of the South. The power and influence of this enterprise can be gauged from the following facts. At the start of the war Fraser, Trenholm's offices at 42 Pine Street, New York, were closed, and the manager, T. Welsman, joined Prioleau, another member of the firm, in Liverpool. To cash in on the blockade-running ventures a branch office was set up in Nassau, under the name of Adderley & Company; John Baptiste Lafitte from Charleston was placed in charge of this venture. Another branch of the firm was opened in Bermuda, and through its branches and contacts the firm assumed the role of international bankers to the Confederacy. C.K. Prioleau was also extremely wealthy, and built a magnificent house at 19 Abercromby Square, Liverpool – the stonework above the front door bearing the 'Bonnie Blue' star of South Carolina.

This was the nature of the company that James Dunwoody Bulloch was instructed to work with. His role, to acquire ships for the Confederacy, was a delicate one, demanding a knowledge of maritime requirements and British and international law. Long before the cruise of the *Sumter* was over the Confederate Government saw that it would be unable to build suitable ships-of-war at home, and took steps to procure them abroad. However, Bulloch, Trenholm, and others were acutely aware that Jefferson Davis had just made the biggest blunder of the war, preventing the Confederacy from obtaining a ready-made fleet of substantial vessels.

At this time the British East India Company was settling its assets, and had for sale, at half price, ten first class Indiamen. Trenholm promptly obtained an option on these, as the total cost of purchasing them and arming them for war was just $2,000,000, worth about 40,000 bales of cotton, when the Confederates had reserves of about 3,000,000 bales. General Beauregard, advised of the situation by Trenholm's son, urged Davis to act without delay but for some reason the Confederate President failed to authorise the purchase. This fleet, had it appeared off Boston, could conceivably have swept the coast from there to the Gulf.

Perhaps because of this blunder, the Confederates now had to move very quickly, and within the parameters of existing laws, if Bulloch and others were to succeed in their missions to provide the Confederacy with an urgently required fleet. Under the rules of international law, even as they stood at this time, ships-of-war were, or should have been, difficult things for a belligerent to obtain from a neutral country. They were on a different footing from other contraband articles. For supplies of ordinary contraband furnished by its subjects, a neutral state was not responsible, the subjects carrying on the trade at their own risk. The view of the Federal Government was that the construction of a belligerent vessel fitted out for purposes of war fell outside the class of acts which foreign subjects might perform consistently with the neutrality of their Governments. According to the rules embodied in the Treaty of Washington, though not then acknowledged by Great Britain to be in force during the Civil War,

"a neutral Government is bound to use due diligence to prevent the fitting out, arming, or equipping within its jurisdiction of any vessel which it has reasonable ground to believe is intended to cruise or carry on any war against a power with which it is at peace; and also to use like diligence to prevent the departure from its jurisdiction of any vessel intended to cruise or to carry on war as above, such vessel having been specially adapted, in whole or in part, with such jurisdiction, to warlike use."

Whether this rule was a part of international law in 1861 or not, a rule somewhat approaching it was generally acknowledged, and found expression in the neutrality laws of different states.(12)

The British statute then in force was the Foreign Enlistment Act, which imposed a penalty for the equipping, furnishing, fitting out, or arming of a vessel with the intent that the vessel should cruise or commit hostilities against a friendly State. "The mere building of a ship within her Majesty's dominions by any person (subject or no subject) is no offence, whatever might be the intent of the parties, because the offence is not the building but the equipping." The enlistment of soldiers, sailors or marines contrary to the provisions of the Act carried a fine of £50 for each such person taken on board. The power given to Customs to seize and detain the ship held good in such an offence only

until the penalty was paid or otherwise secured.(13)

The British Government held that this Act defined the extent of its neutral obligations, a point of view which was to be continually disputed throughout the Civil War by the Federal Government. Had the British Government really wanted to support the Federal Government, and oppose the Confederacy, efforts could have been made to alter the law, but, significantly, no such moves were made.

In their failure to support the North in this manner, the British rulers were inconsistent. The British Government was now foremost in the struggle to oppose slavery, and the slave trade from Africa, and the Government might therefore have been expected to support the United States in this crucial struggle. However, the British Tory establishment also had a profound dislike of democracy. They felt that if the United States experiment in self-rule failed, it might check the agitation for an extension of the electoral reforms of 1832. At this crucial point in American history, notwithstanding the contradictions on the issues of slavery, the British aristocracy were not prepared to alter the aforementioned laws to favour the North, or to shed a great many tears if Lincoln and the Federal Goverment collapsed in their struggle with the Confederacy.

This lack of enthusiasm for the North also had strong economic roots. The blockade was causing British shipping interests to lose money. The threat of curtailed cotton deli-

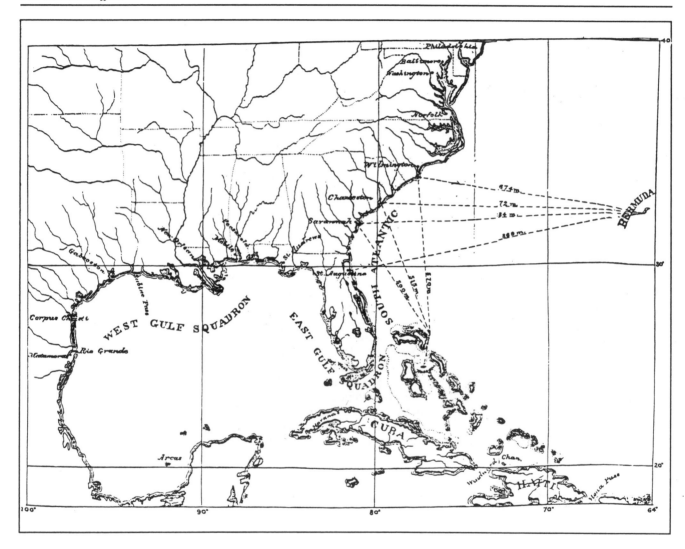

*The Blockaded Coast*

veries to the mills of Lancashire was also a cause of deep resentment in British commercial circles, although the majority of the British working class stood by the North on the anti-slavery principle.

Given this legal and philosophical position, the Confederate agents felt they were safe if they could evade the specific provisions of the Foreign Enlistment Act. This Bulloch and others successfully accomplished by having ships built to full naval specifications, completely prepared for military operations, but lacking their battery, ammunition, and full crew. The vessel could be quickly converted into a fully operational Confederate raider with an arrangement to meet another vessel outside British territorial waters. When the vessels met, guns, equipment and men were transferred, and the vessel became a Confederate man-of-war on the spot. To cover their tracks, agents like Bulloch went through an elaborate legalistic ritual of pretending that they had no links with the Confederacy. Shipbuilders, such as John Laird & Sons, would likewise pose as innocent contractors carrying out a routine order for a private individual, with no knowledge of the true nature or proposed function of the vessel under construction in their yards. This pantomine, however, fooled no one, least of all the Federal authorities or the ordinary citizens of Merseyside.

It was in order to carry out this devious operation that the Confederacy had sent its regularly authorised agents abroad. Besides the Confederate Commissioners, whose mission was primarily diplomatic, these were, first of all, Captain James Dunwoody Bul-

*Jefferson Davis, President of the Confederate States*

loch, and next in importance Fraser, Trenholm & Company. Other agents, with greater or lesser responsibilities, included North and Huse in England, Barron in Paris, Helm in Cuba, Heyliger at Nassau, and Walker at Bermuda. At Liverpool Bulloch was promptly provided with office space by Fraser, Trenholm (with a suitable back entrance to evade the attention of Federal agents) and lost no time in getting down to work.

He at once established contact with William Cowley Miller, a local shipbuilder reputed to have served as shipwright or naval constructor in a British naval dockyard. Miller promptly set to work to build Bulloch a small gunboat, the *Alexandra*, but this vessel was not destined to enter into the services of the Confederacy, for she was detained by the Customs authorities and legal proceedings were instituted while she was being fitted out in the Toxteth Dock in 1862.(14)

Whilst work was in hand on the *Alexandra*, Bulloch was also planning the construction of one of his most successful vessels, the *Florida*, again with Miller & Company, but also in conjunction with Messrs Fawcett Preston & Company of Liverpool – a well known local firm which is still trading today. The financial arrangements were exclusively with Fawcett Preston & Company, who were to build the engines, with Miller & Company building the ship itself. Bulloch and Miller used a plan Miller had of one of Her Majesty's gunboats as a base to start from. They then modified the plans to give her both greater carrying capacity and higher speed. (15)

The contract for this ship was between Bulloch and the builders, and nothing was said about its ultimate destination. But, as even Bulloch had to admit, both contractors must have had a very clear understanding that it would not be very long before the ship they were building would be in the hands of the Confederacy. To hide the true identity of the ship the vessel was given the dockyard name of *Oreto*, and the men working on her were told that she would probably be sent to a mercantile firm doing business with Palermo. It was while negotiations over this vessel were in hand that Bulloch first made his way across the Mersey in order to establish contact with John Laird & Sons.

## John Laird & Sons

The world famous Laird shipbuilding yard at Birkenhead, which Bulloch was about to see for the first time, had been established by the founder, William Laird, in 1824. However, from an early date the yard had been fostered and developed by John Laird, William's eldest son.

By the 1860s the yard had established international fame as pioneer builders of iron vessels. They had produced the first iron vessels for the United States, the first for the navigation of the Indus, Nile, Vistula and Don. In addition to this they had also built the first iron vessels carrying heavy guns – the *Nimrod*, *Nitocrisis*, *Assyria*, *Nemesis*, *Phlegethon*, *Ariadne*, and *Medusa*, all built for the East India Company; and the *Guadeloupe*, for the Mexican Government. The Admiralty's first iron vessel, the *Dover*, was also built there, followed by the steamfrigate *Birkenhead*, of 1,400 tons.

The Laird family name was also well known throughout the world, and particularly in America, due to the activities of John

Laird's younger brother Macgregor. At the age of 23 he had organised, then joined, an expedition to explore the Niger. The loss of life in this famous venture was enormous, Laird himself returning to England more dead than alive. He never lost his interest in Africa, or his love for the African people, becoming a lifelong and very outspoken opponent of slavery.

A few years later Macgregor Laird had joined with Junius Smith and become a director of the British and American Steam Navigation Company. In 1838 their steamer, the *Sirius*, raced across the Atlantic, becoming the first steamer to cross the Western Ocean from England to New York. Competition at this time came from the famous Isambard Kingdom Brunel ship *Great Western*, which they beat by a short head.

After supporting various other explorations to Africa, for which John Laird had built the required ships, Macgregor Laird established another Africa-related shipping venture, the Central Africa Company, an enterprise which evolved into the firm known today as Elder, Dempster & Company. Macgregor Laird, who had given evidence against slavery before two Parliamentary Committees, and corresponded with Wilberforce and the other great abolitionists of the day, died at the early age of 52, on 27 January 1861 -ironically just a few short months before Bulloch, a man dedicated to the perpetuation of slavery, arrived at his brother's yard, seeking practical support for his cause. At this time also John Laird took the decision to hand over the management of the firm to his sons, for Birkenhead had just been made a

parliamentary borough. John set his sights on Westminster, stood for the Conservatives, and was soon to be returned as the first member for Birkenhead. His younger son Henry, already active in the firm in an executive capacity, was also soon to be admitted as a partner.(16)

At the Laird premises Bulloch was given an interesting tour of the yard, and then business commenced. Despite the fact that the firm was particularly noted for the construction of iron ships, Bulloch wanted his vessel made the traditional way – out of wood. The reason for this was that a Confederate raider made of iron would encounter more difficulties when servicing or repair work were required, than one made of wood. Accordingly he soon led the conversation round to the subject of wooden despatch vessels.

The Laird brothers were naturally most interested in the prospect of obtaining an order, giving Bulloch their opinions and the results of their long experience in shipbuilding with enthusiasm. After an hour or so Bulloch shook hands and left, but returned a few days later, asking them if they would be willing to tender for such a vessel, and at the same time giving them all the assurances they required about the funding of the project. A short time after this meeting, when plans and cost had been discussed and agreements finalised, a contract was drawn up for presentation and signatures on 1 August 1861. This was then signed by Henry Laird for the builders and by James Dunwoody Bulloch, ostensibly acting in his own capacity as an intending shipowner. However, as the necessary 'financial assurances' would have had to refer to Fraser, Trenholm & Company, the Laird brothers and John Laird Senior would have been well aware of who the real client was. The agreed specifications also made it clear that they would not be building a merchant vessel, but a man-of-war, complete in every respect for this role, apart from the actual armaments.

The vessel, given the yard number 290, was to be 220 feet long, with a beam of 32 feet, a tonnage of 1040, and two horizontal engines of 300 horse power. She was barque rigged, with very long lower masts, to accommodate exceptionally large fore and aft sails. She was to be admirably fitted out in every respect, the agreement being that only the very best materials would be used; her engines had to be up to Admiralty standards, and the engineer's stores and spare engine-gear on a scale similar to that supplied to a Royal Navy vessel, intending to go on a very long voyage.

In addition to this she was to be provided with condensing apparatus and a cooling tank to supply fresh water. Interestingly she was also to have gun ports – a somewhat unusual feature for an innocent merchant vessel. When finished, according to Bulloch, she was to be "equal to any of Her Majesty's ships of corresponding class in structure and finish, and superior to any vessel of her date in fitness for the purpose of a sea rover, with no home but the sea, and no reliable source of supply but the prizes she might take."(17) The price the Confederates paid Laird & Company for this remarkable vessel was £47,500, payable by the terms of the contract in five equal payments of £9,500 each, and with the last instalment payable after satisfactory trial by Bulloch on the Mersey.

Bulloch was always to maintain later that the Laird family had not the slightest idea of what the ship was intended for, when they agreed to build her. From this point on, the Laird family were to build many ships to aid the cause of the Confederacy, whilst at the same time denying any commercial links with, or commitment to, the Jefferson Davis regime in the Southern states of America. Soon after planning the construction of the *Alabama*, Laird & Sons were planning to build the notorious 'Laird Rams'- the *El Tousson* and the *El Monassir*. They also built the ill-fated Confederate supply ship *Georgiana* (18) and the blockade runners *Wren, Lark, Mary, Robert Todd, Isabel* and *Penguin*. The first two of these runners were not only built by the Laird Brothers, but were the personal property of John Laird Junior! The *Mary* and the *Robert Todd* were owned by the pro-Confederate Liverpool shipowner, Arthur B. Forwood, while the *Penguin* was built to the order of Charles K. Prioleau, one of the partners in Fraser, Trenholm.(19)

## The rival navies

So far as the blockade itself was concerned, Lincoln and the Federal Government now had a monumental task ahead of them, in mounting enough first class ships to give them credibility. The early part of the war was to see blockade running carried on along a coastline thousands of miles long – stretching from the Capes of the Chesapeake in the north to the mighty Rio Grande in the south, all of which had to be patrolled by Federal ships.

In one sense the United States navy was in reasonably good fighting order when the war began, for as soon as the importance of steam as a motive power had been established the early side-wheelers were built: first the *Mississippi* and the *Missouri*, and later the *Powhatan*, *Susquehanna*, and *Saranac*. Next came the six screw-frigates, the *Niagara*, *Roanoke*, *Colorado*, *Merrimac*, *Minnesota*, and *Wabash*. The navy also had many sailing vessels, but as naval science had advanced more between 1835 and 1860 than in the preceding 200 years, more than half the vessels on the navy list had suddenly become useless, and the effective force was narrowed down to the 40 that had steam as a motive power. On the negative side for Lincoln was also the fact that when war broke out the best part of the American fleet was scattered all over the world.

The demands on the new service were many and varied. Ships were required for the river service where the navy supported the army in the reduction of fortified points and in keeping open the lines of communications. Quite distinct from this was the ocean service, which meant the pursuit and capture of Confederate cruisers such as the *Sumter*, *Alabama*, and *Florida*, and vessels engaged in illegal trade. The prime necessity here was speed. Lastly, there was the coast service which maintained the blockade, and detached operations against fortifications

protected by powerful batteries. Operations on the Mississippi alone required a huge fleet, which meant that 40 fully operational, steam powered men-of-war did not go very far. The Federal Government also had a huge mercantile marine trading to all parts of the globe, and needing protection which the navy was unable to provide.

For all these varied functions the United States required a great many ships, in particular for the ocean service, if the threat to their commerce from ships such as the *Sumter*, *Alabama*, and *Florida* were to be countered. Conversely, a few ships served all the requirements of the Confederates, who had virtually no mercantile marine to protect. It would therefore be very easy for a few commerce-raiders to destroy United States merchantmen, which filled the seas, but very difficult to catch the handful of raiders.

## The Sumter and Captain Wilkes

While Bulloch and the Laird brothers were finalising their plans for the construction of the *Alabama*, the man destined to command the vessel was, in the best traditions of piracy, cruising down the Spanish Main, going as far south as Maranham, Brazil, then heading for Martinique. Alas, despite the setting, the pickings for Raphael Semmes in this area were not rich, for in the 55 days between Maranham and Martinique he fell in with only two vessels bearing the flag of the United States. Word was getting round, for the captures and burnings he had accomplished since leaving New Orleans were driving Federal ships off the seas.(20)

On 15 July 1861, the *Sumter* was at the port of St Anne's, Curacoa, where she hoisted the flag of the Confederate States. Permission to enter was withheld until the Governor of the island was assured by Captain Semmes that she was not a privateer, but a ship-of-war. The ship remained eight days in the port and took on coal.(21)

The *Sumter* continued to cruise and destroy until she eventually arrived at St Pierre to coal, but before this work could be completed the United States gunboat *Iroquois* under Captain J.S. Palmer arrived in the harbour. Several times during the night the *Iroquois* steamed around the *Sumter* as if about to open fire, but held back, obviously not wanting to upset the French by mounting an attack whilst in French waters. Leaving nothing to chance, Semmes beat to quarters and ran out his guns.

Captain Palmer, having resisted the considerable temptation to blow Semmes and his crew out of the water, turned to the Governor of Martinique for assistance, protesting about a vessel "engaged in pirating upon the commerce of the United States" being allowed to coal at the port, and asking that she be directed to leave the protection of the French flag. Unfortunately for Palmer, the Governor responded even-handedly, stating that he would not refuse an anchorage to a vessel belonging to the States of the South, and tendering the same hospitalities to the *Iroquois*; but he required the latter, if she

proposed to establish a blockade of the Confederate vessel, to leave the marine jurisdiction of France. To emphasise the point the French man-of-war *Acheron* came round from Port de France, and Palmer was advised that if he remained in the harbour he would not, under international law, be permitted to leave until 24 hours after the departure of the *Sumter*. For nine days Semmes remained blockaded in the port, but eventually made a run for it on the night of 23 October. He steered south and then halted under the shadow of the mountains, which run down abruptly to the sea. The *Iroquois* gave chase, but failed to find the raider.

Having evaded destruction by the *Iroquois*, Semmes' intention now was to cross the Atlantic and cruise in European waters. Off the island of Dominica, on 25 November, he captured the ship *Montmorenci*, and ransomed her on a bond for $20,000, payable to the President of the Confederate States. In all, this voyage across the Atlantic yielded three prizes. Semmes was making a wise choice in moving to a new area, for many United States vessels were now out seaching for him in the waters near the islands of St Thomas and Cuba.

As it happened, one of the half-dozen Federal ships which had been sent to search for the *Sumter* was the screw-sloop *San Jacinto*, commanded by Captain Charles Wilkes. The early months of the Civil War had found Wilkes on duty with the Africa squadron, engaged in the suppression of the slave trade(22) where he would have been working in conjunction with the Royal Navy, then even more active than the United

States Navy in this work. Promptly recalled to fight the Confederates, Wilkes was now heading for a major confrontation with the British.

## A diplomatic incident

It was in October that the *San Jacinto* touched at St Thomas to take on coal. Here for the first time Wilkes learned of the activity of the Confederate raider *Sumter* in those waters. Without delay he set out to search for the enemy. At Cienfuegos, on the south coast of Cuba, he learned that Mason and Slidell, Confederate commissioners to Europe, had recently arrived at Havana from Charleston *en route* to England on board the blockade runner *Theodora*. Wilkes immediately put to sea on 26 October with the purpose of intercepting the *Theodora*. He failed to catch her, but subsequently learned that the Confederate agents planned to embark on 7 November in the English steamer *Trent* for England via St Thomas. Wilkes decided that he would detain the *Trent* and capture the agents, ignoring the international ramifications of such an action.

With this plan in mind Captain Wilkes continued his cruise after the *Sumter* along the north coast of Cuba, also running over to Key West in the hope of finding the *Powhatan* or some other steamer to accompany him to the Bahama channel. Here, 240 miles from Havana, and 90 miles from Sagua la Grande where the channel contracts to the width of 15 miles, at noon on 8 November 1861 the *Trent* was sighted.

As the two vessels drew closer together the *Trent* hoisted English colours, whereupon the United States ensign was hoisted on the *San Jacinto*. The American ship put a shot across the bows of the *Trent*, followed by a further shot which brought her to. The executive officer and a small party from the *San Jacinto* then boarded the English ship and, after many protests, finally managed to take the Confederate agents off the British vessels and onto the United States man-of-war. This action, by Captain Wilkes, was technically a violation of international law; he should have taken the *Trent* to an American port where a prize court would have adjudicated the case. What Captain Wilkes had done, however, was exactly what the British had done scores of times in the early years of the last century – stopped the ships of other nations, searched them, and detained those individuals they were seeking, generally behaving in a high-handed manner towards the ships of other nations.

At first the British government did not hold Wilkes' act contrary to international law. But the mood changed within a few days, when a wave of self-righteous indignation swept over England, or, to be more precise, was orchestrated nationally in the pages of the pro-Confederate Tory press. The British government demanded that the United States release the prisoners and apologise for Captain Wilkes' actions. Orders were issued to hold the fleet in readiness for action, whilst at the same time thousands of British troops were shipped over to Canada, and the export of munitions to America was stopped for a time.(23)

*William Henry Seward,*
*U.S. Secretary of State*

Lincoln and Seward were in a dilemma. If they did not bow to the wishes of Britain, they might have another war on their hands. If they did, American public opinion, which had made a hero out of Wilkes, would be outraged. With much guidance from Lincoln, Seward found a solution to the issue. He did not apologise, but congratulated Britain on at last adopting the principles of international law which the United States had long espoused. Then he had Mason and Slidell shipped off to England. On the whole, American public opinion was pleased; the British were satisfied; and war between the two nations was avoided. In the long run, the *Trent* affair cleared the air; but Britain paid a high price for her insistence on a fine point of law in the lasting seed of resentment that was sown in America.

Other developments in the naval war between the Confederacy and the United States were also to involve Britain at this delicate time. The Confederate raider *Nashville*, a side-wheeler of about 1,300 tons, ran the blockade out of Charleston on the night of 21 October. After stopping for a few days at Bermuda she headed across the Atlantic, and on 19 November captured, in the entrance to the English channel, the ship *Harvey Birch* of New York, homeward bound from Le Havre. The passengers and crew were taken off and paroled and the ship burned. On 21st, the *Nashville* arrived at Southampton, where the prisoners were landed. This vessel had the distinction of being the first war vessel to fly the flag of the Confederate States in the waters of Britain. However, she was soon boxed in by the Federal steamer *Tuscarora*, whose commander, Captain Craven, established such a close watch on the raider that he was warned about a possible breach of neutrality laws. The blockade of the *Nashville* continued during the month; but in the last week of January the *Tuscarora* moved off to the Isle of Wight. At the Confederate commander's request, the Federal ship was detained in British waters for the statutory 24 hours after his own vessel had sailed, and the *Nashville* sailed on 3 February 1862, arriving in Bermuda on the 20th.

# CHAPTER 2

## THE CRUCIAL MONTHS

### John Laird, MP

Whilst events concerning Captain Wilkes and the *Trent* were unfolding in the Atlantic, James Dunwoody Bulloch had been active on Merseyside. For agent Bulloch these were crucial months, as his contractors, the Laird Brothers and Miller & Company, worked to complete the raiders *Alabama* and *Florida*. Other matters took Bulloch away from England during this time, but before leaving England on the *Fingal* in October 1861 he drew up very specific instructions concerning the fitting out of the *Oreto* (*Florida*). His main area of concern was that there should be no violation of the Foreign Enlistment Act. His counsel had explained to him that the ship, when ready for sea, and delivered to him, should be prepared to fulfil the conditions essential to a sea-going steamer – and nothing else! Merseyside did not see James Dunwoody Bulloch again until March 1862. Meanwhile, his main contractor, John Laird, had his mind on other matters.

During the winter of 1861, Birkenhead elected its first Member of Parliament, albeit under a very resticted voting system. The franchise had not yet been extended to include the vast majority of the male working class, while the notion of allowing women to vote was not a matter for serious consideration. With a system rigged to favour the party of the establishment, John Laird stood as the Conservative candidate. However, he faced some notable opposition from Thomas Brassey Junior, standing as a Liberal.

Thomas Brassey Junior was the son of Thomas Brassey, the great railway contractor, who was busy amassing one of the greatest fortunes of the nineteenth century, with thousands of men in his employ. It has been estimated that at certain points in his career Thomas Brassey Senior controlled an army of workers some 80,000 strong. Few, if any, of these men were employed in Birkenhead, a point irrelevant to the pending election, but one that John Laird Senior – in the best tradition of local politicians – made much of during the forthcoming election.

John Laird, described by the local press at the time(1) as a hard and inflexible Tory, was also a Protestant of the fundamentalist variety. Promising to be all things to all men at the hustings, Laird managed to win the support of four Roman Catholic priests to his side, despite his reputation for being on the far right of the Protestant movement then so active on Merseyside. To obtain this support Laird played on the fact that the Liberal party supported the great Italian patriot Garibaldi, who was then struggling to unite Italy, and was thus opposed to the policy of the Vatican. (Within a few months,

Laird was to be the leading light in pro-Garibaldi Protestant riots in Birkenhead!) Amazingly, John Laird also managed to persuade many Liberals to vote for him, some doing so because he was a local man, others because, in their own phraseology, they felt it was "always best to be on the winning side". On the actual day of the election some 20,000 people crowded around the polling station in Birkenhead, to see how the 3,000 with a vote had exercised their privilege. The great contractor's son had put up a good fight for the Liberals, but John Laird received 1,643 votes, with young Thomas Brassey coming a good second with 1,296. On Saturday 14 December, a writer for the local press summed up John Laird's remarkable political stance in these memorable words:

"The new MP for Birkenhead, pliable as he proved to be during his canvas will certainly have a most difficult game to play. He had the support of the Established Church, of the Fosselite Tories, and of the Liberal Conservatives, of personal friends amongst the Liberal party, of men who pretended to believe he was a Liberal, and, finally, of Canon Chapman and the Roman Catholics. If Mr Laird can satisfy the expectations of this heterogeneous combination of supporters, he will prove himself to be more expert in versatility than even his political opponents represent him to be. The web of his Parliamentary life will be one of the most intricate and diversified pieces of workmanship that was ever turned out by political ingenuity. The harlequin who convulses the gods with his double face and figure will be a clumsy buffoon by the side of the Tory MP for Birkenhead. The four heads of Brahma will not suffice for his exigencies."[2]

However, this eloquent writer had underestimated John Laird! At Westminster, his subsequent recorded utterances did little to upset his heterogeneous band of supporters, for, on the infrequent occasions when he spoke, it was invariably about ships (in which commodity he had a vested interest) and little else.

Duly fortified by his democratic triumph at the polls, Laird was now able to concentrate his pliable mind on assisting the undemocratic Confederacy in America. His men, then working on the construction of the *Alabama*, were soon employed in building the infamous 'Laird Rams' for Jefferson Davis – vessels capable of going on the offensive against the Federal Navy.

Meanwhile Fraser, Trenholm & Company, many influential firms connected with the Confederacy, Liverpool merchants, and a diverse collection of mercenary elements were busy at Nassau. Here they had established a blockade-running base; a place where goods could be trans-shipped for onward transmission to ports such as Charleston and Wilmington, past the thin line of Federal warships operating the blockade.

Of the Southern firms, Fraser, Trenholm did the greatest percentage of business at Nassau, as they were not only engaged largely on their own account in blockade-running enterprises, but also acting as agents for the Confederacy. Their representative,

J.B. Lafitte, occupied a prominent position in the local hierarchy, in fact more so than the Colonial Governor himself, and certainly better paid.(3)

Alongside Fraser, Trenholm & Company was the English firm of Collie & Company, which from time to time ran a large fleet of runners mostly commanded by naval officers. One Liverpool firm owned 15 steamers, while a number of small firms owning one or two boats each made the total number of boats and capital employed enormous. The main requirements of the Confederates were war materials of every sort, cloth for uniforms, medicine, salt, boiler-iron, steel, copper, zinc, and chemicals. For those who were prepared to be involved in this trade the profits were huge. The charge for freight at Nassau was £80-£100 per ton in gold. Even ordinary seamen employed on these vessels could earn £50 to £60 for a round trip.(4)

Some idea of the vast profits accruing from blockade running can be gathered by the facts relating to just one Liverpool owned vessel, the *Banshee*. Built by Jones Quiggin

*The blockade runner
'Banshee'*

& Company, she was a 325-ton steel paddle steamer, owned by John T. Lawrence.(5) Thomas Taylor, acting as agent for Lawrence, sailed with her on one of her voyages. He stated that he obtained inward freight at £50 a ton on war materials, and earned in tobacco ballast alone £7,000, the freight for which had been paid at £70 a ton. Coming out they carried 500 bales of cotton, on which they made a profit of £50 per bale – ie £25,000 in total. Without a thought for the cause of slave liberation in the South or the cotton workers of Lancashire, the mercenary Thomas Taylor gleefully recorded his thoughts on his adventurers:

"No wonder I took kindly to my new calling, and no wonder I at once set to work to get the *Banshee* reloaded for another run before the moonless nights were over."(6)

The *Banshee* was eventually captured by the United States Navy, but by this time she had earned sufficient on her eight successful round trips to pay her shareholders an extraordinary 700 per cent return on their investment.

Back in Birkenhead in the winter of 1861, John Laird, basking in his new found status as Member of Parliament for the borough, was busy writing patriotic letters to the press! The '*Trent* Affair' had brought Great Britain to the brink of war with the United States. Notwithstanding the fact that his very own '*Alabama* Affair' would soon be provoking the same threats of war, John Laird was now anxious to ensure that Liverpool would be in a position to repel a 'Yankee' attack should hostilities break out:

"Now that we are spending about a million of money in preparation for war, it may be well to consider in what position Liverpool stands for repelling an attack in the event of a wrestle with America. That some adventurous Yankee, ready to sacrifice everything for fame and the credit of doing a 'smart thing' would 'guess' [sic] his way into Liverpool some dark night, and by means of rockets and inflammable shells endeavour to fire the shipping, is a possibility that must not be overlooked."

As might be expected, the versatile Member of Parliament had many constructive ideas on how to keep the Yankee hordes at bay. He wanted Armstrong guns placed at Rock Perch Battery. He also favoured the establishment of a naval arsenal at the port, the arming of river boats, batteries being placed on the docks, and the construction of earthworks at Crosby, mounted with heavy ordnance.(7)

## Semmes in Europe

Whilst Laird wrote letters Raphael Semmes cruised, eventually bringing his raider into Cadiz on 4 January 1861. On the following day, however, he was ordered by the Military Governor to proceed to sea within 24 hours. Semmes objected, arguing that it was the duty of Spain to extend to his ship the same hospitality that she would extend to the ships of the opposite belligerent; that his vessel was crippled, and that he had 43 prisoners on board, whom he wanted to hand over to the consul of the United States. On orders from Madrid the prisoners were allowed to land, but Semmes was advised to waste no time in leaving the port. He made for Carracca, just eight miles east of Cadiz. Here he was allowed to make repairs that were just sufficient to keep his vessel afloat.

On 17 January Semmes was served with a peremptory order to depart within six hours, and as he had not been permitted to coal he had barely enough fuel to take the ship to the British port of Gibralter, for which he promptly headed. On the way to Gibralter the *Sumter* managed to take two more prizes, one of which was burnt and the other ransomed, having a neutral cargo.(8)

Two days after leaving Carracca the *Sumter* arrived at Gibraltar. Here the American consul at the port immediately informed the Governor by letter, expressing a hope that he would "give such orders as may prevent this rebel cruiser from obtaining the necessary facilities, and making equipments for the continuance of her unlawful vocation". Mr S. Freeling, replying on behalf of the Governor, assured the consul that the British authorities would keep to the letter of the law, so far as the rights and obligations towards both belligerent parties were concerned.

Despite the Governor's efforts to effect an 'even-handed' policy, the *Sumter* was prevented from leaving the port by the actions of the American consul. The consul had in fact succeeded in inducing the merchants of the port not to sell any coal to the Confederate ship, despite the fact that Semmes had been rushing round the port offering 50 per cent more than the market price. In desperation Semmes then tried to obtain coal from the government stores, but this was refused.(9)

By now in something of a flat spin, Semmes hit on the idea of sending his Paymaster, Myers, and Thomas J. Tunstall, by chance ex-United States consul at Gibraltar, to Cadiz, to buy a supply. Alas, luck was not with Raphael Semmes, who was once again outsmarted by a United States consul. The French steamer on which they took passage to Madrid made a stop at the Moorish town of Tangier, where they were arrested by the local authorities on the requisition of the United States consul. He turned them over to the commander of the Federal naval force at Algeciras, who clapped them in irons and sent them off to the United States.

By this time the Federal fleet was homing in on Gibraltar, anxious to settle accounts with Raphael Semmes. On 12 February 1862 the United States war-steamer *Tuscarora* arrived at Gibralter and proceeded to coal at the nearby neutral port of Algeciras. She was soon afterwards joined by the US war-steamer *Ino* and subsequently by the *Kearsage*. These two US ships then waited off Algeciras, in order to intercept the *Sumter*. Blockaded in, and unable to buy coal, Semmes decided, after consultation by telegraph with Mason, to lay her up. All hands were paid off; the officers took passage for London. It was about 13 April 1862 when Semmes set out for England. He then sailed for the Confederacy via Nassau. It was thus whilst he was at the centre of blockade-running activities that he was ordered to return to England, and take command of the *Alabama*.

Mason, with whom Semmes had just conferred over the *Sumter*, had arrived in London with Slidell on 29 January, Slidell at once setting off for Paris. At last in Europe, they were now ready to take up the urgent task of mustering support for the Confederacy in Europe. Mason, the grandson of George Mason of Revolutionary fame, was said to be a man of great personal charm. In Britain he soon found himself overwhelmed with courtesies and social invitations from the pro-Confederate aristocracy.(10)

Apart from selling the dubious 'virtues' of slave power to European Governments, they were both anxious to have the long-heralded opportunity of seeing the power of cotton put to the test. The South hoped that an industrial crisis, created by a cotton famine, would induce Europe to intervene on the side of the Confederacy. While an ultimate crisis was a certainty, nevertheless, the fact that there was not a deep crisis at the time the South had calculated was a serious miscarriage of campaign plans. The simple reason for this was that the large surplus from the abnormally large cotton crops in 1859 and 1860 had ended up in Europe! Nevertheless, by the end of 1861 conditions were certainly getting harder for the mill operatives, with many mills cutting back on operatives' hours of work and pay.

## The birth of the *Florida*

It was at this time, with the blockade-induced crisis just beginning to bite, that James Dunwoody Bulloch arrived back in Liverpool, on 10 March 1862. Bulloch at once made his way to the yard of William C. Miller & Company, where he was delighted to find that the *Oreto* (*Florida*), the first of his Confederate steam-cruisers to be built in England, was ready to take to sea.(11) Others, not so pleased at this prospect, who were also acutely aware that the *Oreto* was ready to sail and had been for some weeks, included the United States consul T.H. Dudley, based in Liverpool. Although he and many others were rightly convinced that the ship was intended for the Confederacy, proving it was another matter, as Bulloch had gone to great pains to cover his tracks.

Firstly, the ship had been registered at the port of Liverpool on 3 March in the name of John Henry Thomas, Merchant of Liverpool. It was also given out that she was being built for the Italian Government. However, concern about the vessel had been mounting during February, to the extent that Charles Francis Adams, American Minister in London, had written a strong note over the issue to Earl Russell, on 18th. In this, he pointed out that the same parties who had dispatched the *Bermuda*, laden with contraband of war, the previous August, were clearly involved with the *Oreto*. This note to Russell was prompted by a letter Adams had received the previous day from Dudley:

"United States Consulate, Liverpool, February 17, 1862

"Sir: The gun-boat *Oreto* is still at this port. She is making a trial trip in the river today.

No armaments as yet on board. She has put up a second smoke stack since I wrote you. She therefore has two funnels, three masts, and is bark-rigged. I am now informed that she is to carry eight rifled cannon, and two long swivel-guns on pivots so arranged to rake both fore and aft. No pains or expense has been spared in her construction, and when fully armed she will be a formidable and dangerous craft. In strength and armament quite equal to the *Tuscarora*; so I should judge from what I learn.

"Mr Miller, who built the hull, says he was employed by Messrs Fawcett, Preston & Co., and that they own the vessel. I have obtained information from many different sources, all of which goes to show that she is intended for the southern confederacy. I am satisfied that this is the case. She is ready to take her arms on board. I cannot learn whether they are to be shipped here or at some other port. Of course she is intended as a privateer. When she sails it will be to burn and destroy whatever she meets with bearing the American flag.

"The *Herald* sailed for Charleston on Saturday last; Captain Coxeter went out in her. The *Bermuda* will sail this week.

"I have, &c.,( Signed ) H. Dudley, United States Consul.

"P.S.- The gun-carriages for the *Oreto*, I have just learned, were taken on board on Friday night last, in a rough state, and taken down into the hold. Fraser, Trenholm & Co. have made advances to Fawcett, Preston & Co., and Miller, the builder. H.D."

Both Dudley and Adams were well aware that the ship would leave Liverpool without actually putting ammunition and arms on board, but would in all probability run into some small port where this could easily be

*Charles Francis Adams, United States Minister, London*

done. Dudley also checked out the story regarding the final owners of the ship. The Italian consul at Liverpool informed him that he knew nothing about it, and had no knowledge whatsoever of any vessel being built for his Government.(12) However, representations made to the Foreign Office were to no effect, and plans for her departure went smoothly ahead.(13)

Captain James Alexander Duguid was appointed to command the ship, and a crew was recruited, according to Bulloch, in strict accordance with the law, so that no infringement of the Foreign Enlistment Act had been made. She sailed from Liverpool on 22 March 1862, having on board Master John Lowe, CSN, who was instructed to deliver the vessel to Captain J.N. Maffitt at Nassau. The actual agents for the ship at this base were Adderly & Company, the Nassau correspondent of Fraser, Trenholm & Company.

At about the same time that the *Oreto* left Liverpool another ship, the steamer *Bahama*, had set sail from Hartlepool, also bound for Nassau. In her holds were all the guns and ammunition required to convert the *Oreto* into the Confederate man-of-war *Florida*. Her battery in fact consisting of two seven-inch rifles and six 6-inch guns, with carriages and ammunition.(14)

After a passage of 37 days the *Florida* arrived at Nassau on 28 April, Lowe reporting to Bulloch that in compliance with his instructions the voyage out had been made principally under canvas, to save coal. Lowe was most happy to report that the ship behaved well under both steam and canvas, and that under favourable conditions, with both sail and steam in use, they could make up to 13 knots.

Lieutenant James Newland Maffitt was subsequently placed in command of the ship, with Lieutenant Samuel W. Averett acting as his 1st Officer. Averett had graduated from the US Naval Academy in 1859, then served in the Pacific squadron until about 1 April 1861, when he had resigned with the intention of serving the Confederacy. Other officers of the ship were J.L. Hoole, C.W. Read, and S.G. Stone.(15)

With her officers and crew on board the vessel was taken down the coast to Cochrane's Anchorage, an inlet some nine miles from Nassau, where she took on board her arms and ammunition. The aim was to accomplish the delicate operation of converting her from an unarmed ship to a fully armed cruiser – in British waters – out of sight, and without legal complications. However, this task was soon discontinued, as it was belatedly recognised that it would leave no loophole for the authorities to ignore the character of the vessel.

During this time, and later, she was inspected officially by British naval officers, who not surprisingly reported that she was in every way fitted out as a man-of-war, remarkably similar to a despatch gun-vessel in Her Majesty's service. This was no coincidence, as her builder, Miller of Liverpool, had borrowed a plan of just such a vessel in order to build her to these high naval standards. To add to the troubles of the

Confederates she was then deserted by most of her crew, on the reasonable grounds that they did not wish to fight for the Confederacy. A new crew therefore had to be rounded up and shipped at Nassau.

All the above activity was noted by the British colonial authority, and the *Oreto* was libelled in the Vice-Admiralty Court. As might be expected, however, in a British colony then making a fortune out of pro-Confederacy activity, the trial did not reflect well upon the character of judicial proceedings there. The vessel was released on 7 August and sailed on the same day under Maffitt's command for Green Cay, an uninhabited island in the Bahamas. At the same time the armaments for the cruiser were placed on a schooner, which the *Oreto* met at Green Cay on 10 August. There the arms were transferred to the cruiser, which was then regularly commissioned as a ship-of-war. The Confederate flag was hoisted, and the name changed to *Florida*. But as we shall see, more troubles lay ahead for Maffitt and his crew.

## The cotton crisis in England

Whilst those engaged in pro-Confederate activity on Merseyside made money, others began to suffer as a direct result of the cotton famine, which was now starting to bite. At the annual meeting of the District Provident Society, held in Liverpool on 13 March, the Mayor, Robert Hutchison, reported that for some time now the cotton porters had been reduced to dire straits by the greatly reduced import of cotton, which had been countered to a degree by an increase in the arrival of grain-laden vessels. However, this was not enough to stave off real hardship; many hands were now idle, and to a large extent augmenting the amount of destitution in the town. To meet this situation soup kitchens were opened in different parts of the town, by which means a large amount of relief was afforded.(16)

There were also increasing signs of a deepening crisis in the Lancashire mill towns, being felt more in Blackburn than any other town in the country. Dire poverty had now desolated many comfortable homes, bringing even the most careful of the operatives to seek relief from the public relief fund, or the parochial rates. On 24 March figures from the local Board of Guardians showed that 9,610 persons were relieved from absolute want, 280 more than the previous week, and 6,976 more than during the same week in 1861. 6,000 operatives were now unemployed in this town alone. The compassionate Guardians could only find employment for 400 of this number, at 1s 6d per day.(17)

Despite all this suffering, one section of the Liverpool press reported that the line being peddled in the area by pro-Confederate elements was still being rejected by the workers. This line was that England or France should interpose, induce the North to recognise the independence of the South, and end the war. America would have peace, England cotton, and Lancashire artisans bread. However, the reporter was pleased to record that this pro-Confederate propaganda had not deluded one single cotton operative.

It was, the reporter noted, the pet scheme of Liverpool advocates of the Southern cause, and of such flippant and half-informed, inflated persons as Mr Spence, the author of a pro-Confederate booklet. He continued that it was an encouraging and proud reflection that none of those appeals for intervention had come from the very class on whose behalf most people professed to claim it – the operatives of Lancashire:

"Call a monster meeting of the spinners of the county to-morrow, and you will find that such suggestions will be rejected with as much contempt as we show to them now. We have all good reason to be proud of the Lancashire operatives. They at least are not the ignorant, stupid, selfish sots Mr Roebuck painted, as specimens of the English artisan, a short time since."

The article concluded by pointing out that many mill owners, whose profits were suspended, were dipping into their dwindling funds to help their destitute workers, but many more were clearly not, and it was their duty to stand by their poor impoverished workers in such hard times.(18)

## Completing the *Alabama*

With the Confederate ship *Florida* safely away on the high seas, Bulloch now concentrated all his attention on the *Alabama*, still under construction at Birkenhead. The attention of others was also concentrated on this vessel, namely Dudley, the United States consul in Liverpool, and Charles Francis Adams, the American Minister in London –

both of whom were well aware for whom the ship was being built. Dudley's spies were now highly active, watching developments at Birkenhead, whilst a private detective by the name of Maguire, hired by the consul, watched every move that Bulloch made.

However, work on the ship continued, and as the vessel neared completion Bulloch made plans to hire a captain who would be willing to assume initial command of the vessel and take her out of British waters. He consulted with a friend over this matter, who suggested that the right man for this delicate task was a Captain J. Butcher, who was then serving as 1st Officer on a Cunard steamship but held a Master's Certificate, and was therefore suitable for the job.

A short conversation between Bulloch and Butcher brought matters to a satisfactory conclusion, although exactly how much money Bulloch had to offer Butcher to induce him to leave Cunard for a short-term and risky engagement with the Confederacy is not recorded. One imagines that it must have been a substantial amount. According to Bulloch, it was made clear to Butcher that he had been engaged merely to take the ship to a foreign port; and he was supposedly warned that no men must be engaged, under any pretext whatsoever, except as crew to get the vessel to a port in the West Indies.

Bulloch subsequently went to great pains to emphasise that no men were hired as crew for this ship other than for the purpose of taking an unarmed ship out of Liverpool, and that no man was enlisted at the port with a view to entering the services of the Confederacy. However, as it was by now common knowledge on Merseyside that the ship was being built for the Confederate states and that Bulloch was acting as agent for the venture, no one who signed up with Butcher to crew the '290' would have been unaware of what they were doing.

The vessel was eventually launched on 15 May 1862, being christened the *Enrica* by a 'Christian Lady', who Bulloch also claimed had no idea of her part in the Civil War. Merseyside, it would seem, was bursting at the seams with gullible people.(19)

As soon as the ship was in the water two tugs took her in tow, and she was taken to the graving-dock, warped in, and placed over the blocks at once. Attempts were being made to detain the ship, and aware of these the Laird brothers made great efforts to complete the ship and get her away. An indication of this haste can be gained from the fact that even before the *Enrica* was fully secured in her berth after the launch, the great derricks swung out over her decks and the first pieces of heavy machinery were put on board. Exactly one month after being launched the ship was completed, and a satisfactory trial trip was made on 15 June.

On 21 June Dudley wrote to Adams informing him of developments on Merseyside. He felt that there was no room to doubt the fact that the vessel just launched at Birkenhead was about to enter the service of the Confederacy. Amongst the information that he obtained was a statement from Beaufort and Caddy, two of the officers from the

privateer *Sumter*, who stated that the vessel was definitely being built for the Confederate states. The foreman at Laird's yard had also stuck his neck out, informing Dudley that the '290' had been built as a sister ship to the gun-boat *Oreto*, and had been built for the same parties and for the same purpose; when pressed he confirmed

*Captain James Dunwoody Bulloch, Confederate States main agent in England*

southern government in the United States. Added to this, Dudley had even been able to extract information from the captain and officers of the steamer *Julia Usher*, a blockade runner, who confirmed that the gun-boat was built for the Confederacy and was to be commanded by Bulloch.(20)

This information prompted Charles Francis Adams to write to Earl Russell on 23 June, pointing out that an even more powerful steamer than the *Oreto* had been built at the yard of a person then sitting as a member of the House of Commons, and was fitting out to carry on hostilities against the United States. He concluded his note:

"I now ask permission to transmit, for your consideration, a letter addressed to me by the consul of the United States at Liverpool, in confirmation of the statements here submitted, and to solicit such action as may tend either to stop the projected expedition, or to establish the fact that its purpose is not inimical to the people of the United States."(21)

In a letter from the Foreign Office dated 25 June, Russell informed Adams that he had lost no time in referring the matter to the proper department of Her Majesty's Government. On the same day an official at the Foreign Office, E. Hammond, wrote to the Secretary of the Treasury, requesting that immediate inquiries be made respecting the vessel, and to take such steps as might be right and proper. Hammond then wrote to the Law Officers of the Crown, giving them all the information on the issue and asking them to favour Lord Russell with any observations they might have upon the question. Subsequent developments would also seem to indicate that pro-Confederate elements at the Foreign Office leaked information to Bulloch at this crucial juncture.

The information Dudley had received about Bulloch being given command of the ship was wrong. Although it had been the original intention of the Confederacy to give him command, a despatch received by Bulloch at the last moment informed him that Captain Semmes was returning to England from Nassau, and was to be given command of the ship. At the same time Bulloch received a letter from Semmes himself, advising that he would join him in Liverpool by the first vessel leaving Nassau. Bulloch found this change in plans "embarrassing", coming so late, for by then he knew that Adams was pressing the Government to seize the ship.

The watchfulness of the Customs officers at Liverpool, apart from any possible 'leaks' from London, was also beginning to worry Bulloch. Now extremely concerned, he instructed his men to get the *Enrica* into Birkenhead Dock, where she was coaled and all her stores put on board. Everything was now put on 'Red Alert' pending a rapid departure from the Mersey. However, a full crew could not be shipped, for Bulloch knew the men might become restive at the delay and attract notice by their numbers and 'indiscreet talking' – an interesting contradiction of Bulloch's earlier assertions of their innocence. Subsequent developments indicate that they all had a very clear understanding of the venture.

indicate that they all had a very clear understanding of the venture.

## The *Enrica* departs

The ship sailed from Liverpool on 29 July 1862, some three or four days earlier than planned, because of the ever increasing possibility that pressure from the United States would prevent her leaving.

Clarence R. Yonge, one of the crew, later gave a very interesting account of events surrounding her departure. Yonge, who had been engaged as Paymaster, was instructed by Bulloch to report to Fraser, Trenholm's office on the morning of Monday 28 July. Here he was informed that the ship would sail the next day. He went on board on Tuesday morning, and the ship started to move down the river at about 10.30am. All on board were well aware that there was no intention of returning, although a cover story had been put around that this trip was merely a further trial run.

On board at this time were a party of guests to give substance to the cover story, who included the two older Laird brothers, John and William, and two of their sisters. On coming on board one of the Laird brothers gave Yonge a substantial sum of money, which he understood to be the balance of money left after he had made numerous purchases for Bulloch. All this indicates how deeply involved the Laird family were in efforts to get the Confederate vessel away, and evade the attention of the law officers. In the afternoon the Laird family and some other guests were transferred to an accompanying steam-tug, which took then back to Liverpool. The vessel then ran down to Moelfra Bay, and lay there all that night.(22)

As soon as it had become evident that the cruiser had escaped from the Mersey the United States officers at Liverpool telegraphed the Federal steamer *Tuscarora*, then cruising off the south-western shores of Britain. She made all haste to get to the area, but failed to find the *Enrica*, which was fortunate for the Confederates; had she done so the *Enrica*'s career would certainly have terminated there and then, as she still had no armaments on board. After spending the night at Moelfra she made her way to the Atlantic through the North Channel, in a deliberate and successful attempt to evade the attention of the *Tuscarora* and other Federal ships. Once out in the Atlantic, Captain Butcher steered for the Azores, at an average speed of 13.5 knots an hour.(23) She duly arrived at Terceira on 10 August, declaring herself to be the *Barcelona*, built for the Spanish Government and destined to be a cruiser in Mexican waters.

At the Azores the *Enrica* was shortly to be joined by the barque *Agrippina*, the vessel Bulloch had obtained to act as tender to his raider. When Bulloch bought this vessel in London in May he had found it easy to get her loaded with stores, and all the armaments and ammunition that would convert the *Enrica* into the Confederate raider *Alabama*, without arousing any suspicion. Captain Alexander McQueen was given command of the vessel by Bulloch.

It was when it had become clear to Bulloch that he had to get the *Enrica* away from Liverpool without delay that he telegraphed the agents who were loading the *Agrippina* in London to get her away forthwith. At the same time he gave very detailed instructions to McQueen. He was to make his way to the Bay of Praya, in the island of Terceira, to link up with Butcher and the *Enrica*. He was then to work closely with the master of the *Enrica* in getting all the stores, coal, ammunition, and guns etc, moved from his ship to the raider.(24)

Bulloch wrote many letters at this time, including one to Acting Assistant-Paymaster C.R. Yonge. Anxious to recruit as many men on board the ship as possible to the Confederate service, Bulloch instructed Yonge:

"When the *Alabama* is fairly at sea you will mix freely with the warrant and petty officers, show interest in their comfort and welfare, and endeavour to excite their interest in the approaching cruise of the ship. Talk to them of the Southern States, and how they are fighting against great odds for only what every Englishman enjoys – liberty!"

Bulloch also advised him that when Captain Semmes joined he was to act under his instructions, and to "smooth his way" by having all the ship's stores and cargo in an orderly state, and the men well settled, by the time Semmes arrived.

## Semmes joins the *Alabama*

Captain Raphael Semmes arrived in Liverpool on 8 August on the steamer *Bahama* from Nassau, where he spent a few busy days gathering his old officers on the *Sumter* around him, and making financial arrangements for the cruise with Fraser, Trenholm & Company. Arrangements completed, he, with Bulloch and others, sailed from Liverpool on the same vessel, bound for the Azores, on 13 August, arriving at Praya on 20th. After much coming and going between the *Bahama* and the *Alabama*, Semmes arrived back on the *Bahama* on Sunday 24 August, where he at once called all the men under the bridge, with himself and the officers standing above. According to one of the men, John Lathom, of Liverpool, he said:

"Now, my lads, there is the ship" [pointing to the *Alabama*]; "She is as fine a vessel as ever floated; there is a chance which seldom offers itself to a British seaman, that is to make a little money. I am not going to put you alongside of a frigate at first; but after I have got you drilled a little, I will give you a nice fight.... There is only six ships that I am afraid of in the United States Navy.... We are going to burn sink and destroy the commerce of the United States; your prize money will be divided proportionately according to each man's rank, something similar to the English Navy."

Raphael Semmes then pointed to Kell, his 1st Officer, standing on the deck, informing the men that if they wished to sign up for this venture, they were to go aft and give him their names. A great many reflected on found that a great many of the men who had already signed up for the cruise were those that had gone aboard her at Liverpool.

As soon as the men who had consented to go had all signed articles, the English ensign, which the *Alabama* had been flying, was pulled down, the Confederate flag hoisted, and a gun fired. The men who had declined to sign up left the ship with Captains Bulloch and Butcher, and headed for the Bahamas, and back to the relative safety of Liverpool.(26)

In their interminable accounts of matters relating to the *Alabama*, both Semmes and Bulloch skate very lightly over the place and timing of the actual enlistment process for this cruise. Semmes merely states that all the men on board the *Alabama* and those who had come out with him in the *Bahama* had been brought thus far under articles that were no longer obligatory; they had certainly not signed for service on board a Confederate cruiser, to avoid a breach of the British Foreign Enlistment Act:

"They had, of course, been undeceived from the day of our departure from Liverpool. They knew that they were to be released from the contracts they had made, but I could not know how many of them would engage with me for the *Alabama*. It is true I had a talk with some of the leaders of the crew, who had promised to go with me, and to influence others, but no creature can be more whimsical than a sailor, until you have bound him past recall, unless indeed it be a woman."(27)

Semmes makes no mention of an actual recruiting speech, although Lathom's account of events on board the *Bahama* rings true. Nor does Semmes state what was said when he spoke to "some of the leaders of the crew", or if others besides himself had influenced these men to sail for the Confederates back in Liverpool. In fact, many of the men, such as William Passmore, and 30 others who had signed up in Laird's shipyard, were fully aware that she was going out as a Southern cruiser, and subsequent statements made under oath from such men were to later tip the balance in favour of America in the international dispute relating to Britain's position as a neutral nation, and cited as an infringement of the Foreign Enlistment Act.

Amongst the mainly American officers of the *Alabama* was J.M. Kell, another true son of the 'Deep South' whose influential family were amongst the slave-owning plantocracy of the Confederate States. He saw the cause of the South as a noble one, in which his 'mother country' was struggling for freedom against the Union. Francis L. Galt from Virginia was the surgeon, who later served as paymaster after Semmes and Clarence Yonge had parted company. Irvine S. Bulloch, brother of Captain James Dunwoody Bulloch, shipped as a midshipman, but later acted as sailing master, and R.K. Howell, brother-in-law of Confederate President Jefferson Davies, sailed as the 'Lieutenant of Marines' -despite the fact that no marines were actually carried! Other officers with 'social connections', who sailed with the ship were Eugene Maffitt, Captain Maffitt's son, and Edward Maffitt Anderson, son of brother-in-law of Confederate President Jefferson Davies, sailed as the 'Lieutenant of Marines' -despite the fact that no marines were actually carried! Other officers with 'social connections', who sailed with the ship were Eugene Maffitt, Captain Maffitt's son, and Edward Maffitt Anderson, son of Colonel Anderson. So far as the crew were concerned, none of them were American; virtually all were British, and most from Liverpool.(28)

On the morning of Sunday 24 August, the *Alabama* sailed away from the picturesque island of Terceira. Under a cloudless sky, and with the corn fields and orange groves of the island in the distant background, the flag of the new-born Confederate States was unfurled from the peak of the *Alabama* for the first time (according to Semmes) and fluttered in the light breeze. So it was that a ship, built in a British shipyard and almost entirely crewed by British seamen, set sail on a mission of destruction against the interests of the United States under the Presidency of Abraham Lincoln. As they sailed away in the interests of Jefferson Davis, the ship's band played the 'soul-stirring' anthem of the new-born government, 'Dixie', whilst the *Bahama* fired a gun and cheered the new flag. When the two vessels parted off the island of Terceira, Bulloch arranged with Semmes that he would send out the *Agrippina* to him with a cargo of coals and other supplies, and the barque was accordingly ordered to go to Cardiff to load. Semmes was instructed to meet up with his tender at St Pierre in the

French island of Martinique, on an agreed date.(29)

No time was lost in commencing offensive operations against the Federal merchant marine. Just five days after leaving Terceira a Federal brig was spotted and chased, but escaped in the darkness of the night. A whaling schooner, the *Ocmulgee* from Martha's Vineyard, one of the islands of Massachusetts, was destined to be the first victim of the *Alabama*. The fact that she was from New England, where there was a traditional religious opposition to slavery, must have been rather gratifying to Semmes. The voyage of the *Ocmulgee* had been a very successful one, as she had a good store of whale oil on board, ship and cargo being later valued at $131,712.00. On 5 September the boats of the raider came up to the unarmed vessel, took possession of her, and declared her officers and crew prisoners. The next day the ship and cargo were burnt, and the captive crew placed in irons by Semmes. The long and destructive cruise of the Confederate raider *Alabama* had begun.

# CHAPTER 3

## FAMINE AND DESTRUCTION

### Crisis in England

When the *Alabama* sailed from Liverpool in July 1862, the national and local press were carrying long and moving accounts of the distress in the cotton districts. The Cotton Famine was beginning to bite, and bite hard. It was now clear that the diminution of the cotton stocks would lead to more mill closures, adding to the already horrendous suffering of the unemployed cotton operatives.

In Ashton-under-Lyne 9,600 were now living on the rates. In Blackburn the numbers were 10,600 in the last week of May, which rose to 11,500 by the last week in June. In Manchester, over the same period, numbers rose from 12,700 to 14,200; in Preston, from 11,800 to 12,100; and in Stockport from 5,400 to 6,000.

In Burnley, for instance, where there were 13,000 operatives, there were 10,000 out of employment, who were not receiving parish relief. The returns of the number of 'paupers' therefore give no adequate measure of the staggering amount of distress and suffering which prevailed. How were they managing to survive? The reporter for *The Times* discovered that money withdrawn by operatives from savings accounts came to a total of £4,500, and from Building Societies to £3,700, while during the same period they received from voluntary contributions the paltry sum of £458. It was clear, therefore, that these proud workers were animated by a strong desire to preserve their independence – and keep away from the clutches of the dreaded workhouse masters.

The liability of the separate parishes was not adjusted to the huge burden which some were now having to bear. The parochial division of the country was not geared to deal with the support of the poor in such a mass crisis, as it was a division for ecclesiastical purposes. In theory, other parishes were legally obliged to assist those in desperate straits. In practice, however, distress was on the increase generally, and external support commensurate with the situation was not getting through to those who were suffering.

In the House, the MP Gilpin stated that although he did not wish to represent the situation too darkly, it would be difficult to paint too black a picture:

"The sufferings hitherto endured by the poor operatives were bad enough, but they were as nothing as compared with the probable amount of poverty and destitution which would come upon Lancashire during the winter."[1]

The British Government had by now decided to organise some relief on a national scale and, on the opposite side of the Atlantic, so had the Federal Government of President Abraham Lincoln, which organised the dispatch of relief ships to England. One of these vessels was the *Brilliant*, which left America in September 1862 laden with flour and corn for the starving mill operatives of Lancashire. Together the ship and cargo were valued at $164,000. Unfortunately, she was captured by Captain Raphael Semmes on 3 October, and burnt and destroyed. Semmes stated later that, although it went to his heart to destroy her and her cargo, he had no alternative, and his duty to his government compelled him to burn her.(2)

## Semmes scores

Semmes had in fact had a busy month since his active career as master of the *Alabama* began with the destruction of the *Ocmulgee* on 5 September. On 7th he had destroyed the merchant schooner *Starlight*, valued at $4,000, and on 8th he found another helpless victim, the whaling barque *Ocean Rover* – a much more valuable catch, ship and cargo being worth $98,820; she too was rapidly sent to the bottom of the ocean. 9 September was a particularly good day for Semmes, the catch being two more whalers, the *Alert* and the *Weather Gauge*, worth $52,000 and $10,000 respectively. Between this date and his encounter with the relief ship *Brilliant*, Semmes found and destroyed five more whalers – the *Attamaha*, *Benjamin Tucker*, *Courser*, *Virginia*, and *Elisha Dunbar*. So far as senseless destruction was concerned this was a marvellous score, but not one that

would qualify Semmes for recognition as a naval hero – all his victims having been nothing more than proverbial 'sitting ducks.'

Semmes was no fool, however, and well understood his role as a destroyer of commerce. His previous cruise in the *Sumter* had given him invaluable experience, and he therefore entered upon the cruise of the *Alabama* with a well-considered plan of operations. He made a careful study of the ocean routes used by Federal shipping and planned accordingly, locating his ship at strategic striking points.

He also worked out how long news of his presence in a given area would take to reach the United States, and before a worthy adversary could arrive to blow him out of the water, moved on to a new scene of operation. The maximum period he allowed himself in any one area was about two months. By then he and his crew would be well on their way to another cruising ground. He passed his first two months in the North Atlantic, before moving south to his new cruising ground. After leaving the West Indies he moved south, posting himself strategically near the equator, right in the track of South American commerce.(3)

One encounter which gave particular satisfaction to Semmes related to the capture of the brig *Dunkirk*, which he found and destroyed on 7 October. After taking the crew prisoner, he found that one of them, a man by the name of Forrest, had served with him on the *Sumter*, but had deserted the vessel at Cadiz. A few days later Semmes, playing the role of judge, jury, and executioner, had him tried as a deserter from the naval service of the Confederate Government. Predictably, Semmes found him guilty, and sentenced him to lose all title to wages – and prize money due to him. However, this was not a very shrewd move by Semmes, because from the moment of his condemnation Forrest did his level best to incite the rest of the crew to mutiny.

On 15 October the *Alabama* captured and destroyed the Federal ship *Lamplighter*, which was valued at $117,600 – one of the raider's more spectacular catches. The following day, however, the *Alabama* herself was in grave danger of joining the growing list of ships she had sent to the bottom of the sea, when a terrific gale put her qualities as a sea-going vessel to the test. The Laird-built vessel survived, but suffered severe damage, which compelled her to lie to for some days, until 23rd of the month when, fully recovered, she attacked and sank two vessels of the same name, the ship *Lafayette* valued at $110,337, and the smaller barque *Lafayette*, worth just $36,025.(4)

## The trials of the *Florida*

Whilst the *Alabama* had got off to a notable start in her career as a commerce destroyer, Captain Maffitt was continuing to have nothing but bad luck with his Merseyside-built vessel, the *Florida*. After he had taken on his armaments at Green Cay on 10 August, yellow fever broke out amongst his small crew of 18 men, and in five days the work force was reduced to one fireman and four deck hands. In desperation Maffitt ran

into Cardenas, Cuba, and was himself stricken with the disease. Whilst he was still seriously ill, the *Florida* was summoned to Havana by the Captain General. The ship itself was still far from being fully equipped or manned, and because Maffitt was concerned over the stringency of Spanish regulations he decided to make a run for Mobile – despite the risk involved in getting past the line of blockading Federal warships.(5)

On 4 September she was off the bar, where she found three Federal warships blocking the way into the port. His options at this point being extremely limited, Maffitt hoisted the British colours and stood toward the three warships. The Federal ships then allowed the *Florida* to come up to them, before ordering her to stop. Maffitt responded by substituting the Confederate flag for the British flag. The Federal sloop-of-war *Oneida* replied with a huge broadside, and continued this treatment for the next two hours. Two shells passed right through the *Florida*, and considerable damage was done to her masts and rigging, but she eventually found shelter under the Confederate guns of Fort Morgan.

It was here, whilst the ship was in quarantine, that Lieutenant Stribling was attacked with fever and died. Under the disadvantage of being an infected ship and remote from the workshops, efforts were made to repair the raider and complete her equipment. In the meantime the blockading squadron had been increased, the Federal navy being well aware of how much damage such a vessel could do to their merchant marine, once at large on the high seas. Maffitt decided to wait until winter before attempting to escape. He remained here until 15 January 1863.

## The efforts of Admiral Wilkes

By now the Federal Government was increasingly worried by the activity of the *Alabama*, and the potential threat of the *Florida* and other raiders. Accordingly, orders were issued on 8 September creating the West Indies Squadron, consisting of seven third-class cruisers. In weight, metal and speed, only two of these equalled the *Alabama* or the *Florida*. Acting Rear-Admiral Wilkes was assigned to the command of this squadron. Of the seven ships assigned to him, only three were component parts of the Potomac River Flotilla; the other four were to be detached from various commands and join him in the West Indies.(6)

The instructions given to Wilkes designated the West Indies and the Bahamas as the cruising ground, the actual ships placed at his disposal consisting of the sloops-of-war *Wachusett* and *Dacotah*, the double-enders

*Wilkes' operations, 1861-63*

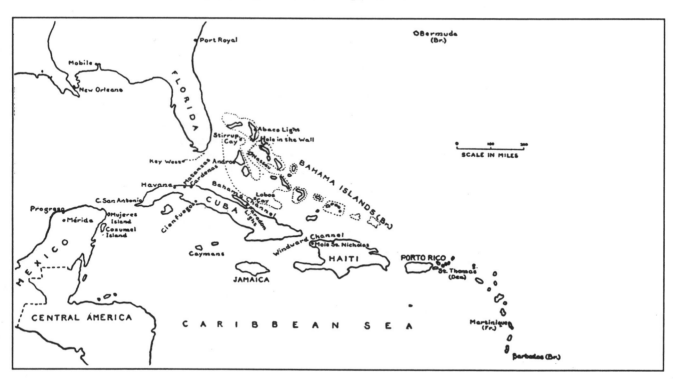

*Cimmerone*, *Sonoma*, *Tioga* and *Octorara*, and the fast side-wheel steamer *Santiago de Cuba*. Of this squadron the two vessels fitted to cope singly with the *Alabama* were the *Wachusett* and the *Dacotah*.

Wilkes sailed from Hampton Roads in the *Wachusett* on 24 September with the nucleus of his squadron, the seven-gun *Sonoma* and the eight-gun *Tioga*. On the afternoon of 27 September the three vessels arrived off St George, Bermuda. The *Sonoma* was ordered to cruise off the coast, while the *Wachusett* and the *Tioga* went into port to obtain coal, supplies, and minor repairs.

The rather abrasive Wilkes immediately got into a row with Colonel Ord, the British Governor. No English ensign had been shown when the American warships had entered the harbour and, to add insult to injury, a representative of the Governor who came aboard the *Wachusett*, was a person in ordinary dress and not identifiable as an official. The insult was most probably a deliberate and calculated one as this particular colony, then making a fortune out of blockade-running, would hardly have been pleased to see the arrival of Wilkes and his Federal squadron.

The Admiral's ire was understandably aroused still more by the presence of seven English steamers, obviously blockade runners, the Captains of which even boasted on shore "that they were engaged in illicit or contraband trade with the rebels". So far as the non-display of the English ensign was concerned he managed to obtain an apology from Lieutenant Colonel Munro, who attri-

buted it to the negligence of the guard detail and assured the Admiral that proper disciplinary measures had been taken. The flag was then displayed and national salutes followed.

Altogether Wilkes was to have a total of 16 vessels under his command. He made some captures of neutral vessels engaged in contraband trade, and from time to time worried English steamers in the West Indies, ruffling many feathers on the far side of the Atlantic in the process. He also incurred the displeasure of the Federal Government by several unwarranted acts, particularly the retention of vessels, as part of his command, which belonged to other squadrons, or had been ordered on special service.

After the *Alabama* had reached the West Indies in November 1862, it was appreciated by the Federal navy that she would not remain long in that area. Efforts were increased to catch the raider at this point by fitting out the *Vanderbilt*, one of the fastest steamers in the navy which, under the command of Commander Baldwin, was sent on a roving commission in the direction which the *Alabama* was expected to head for. Although this vessel was operating under a separate command, Wilkes made the mistake of exceeding his authority by detaining her (see Chapter 4), and in consequences of this and other misdemeanours he was to be relieved in June 1863 by Commodore Lardner.

## The effect on Britain

In England during August 1862, the crisis caused by the cotton famine was worsening. Fears were now mounting among some politicians that the crisis could even develop into a revolution. A general turnout of unemployed cotton operatives was expected at Oldham on 11 August, when they proposed to go to the mills that were still working and draw the boiler plugs, as in 1842 when the Chartists activated workers to do this and managed to stop all the mills. Some of the workers believed that the high price of cotton was the cause of unemployment, and that a general stoppage, by bringing down the price of cotton, would cure the problem. This simple, but unrealistic, proposition, failed to win over the operatives; groups of people did begin to assemble in the streets at an early hour, but they did not proceed to march to the mills.(7)

However, it was an article of faith with some Southern leaders that 'Cotton was King'. This was one reason why Semmes sank the relief ship *Brilliant*, an action which could only have the direct and immediate effect of heightening the crisis in the mill towns, and putting pressure on the British Government. The Southern theory was that Britain and France in particular, deprived of Southern cotton and facing social unrest, would of necessity intervene to break the blockade and thus assure Southern victory. Even if Britain did not go this far, she would surely rally European opinion to force mediation upon the North, which would almost certainly assure Southern independence – and the continuation of the slave system in America.

Again and again, Britain did seem to be on the verge of some kind of recognition or intervention, particularly at the time of the '*Trent* Affair' and again in the summer of 1862, just 18 days after the potential crisis in Oldham, this time prompted by General Robert E. Lee's victories in Virginia.(8)

It had been on 2 July that President Lincoln issued a proclamation calling for 300,000 more volunteers. General Halleck was now in command of all the Union armies in the field. General McClellan was ordered to leave the James river, and take his forces to the Potomac, to join them to the army under Pope. Lee, no longer fearing for Richmond, now hastened to attack Pope, who commanded the Union forces in Virginia. Jackson defeated Pope's right wing at Cedar Mountain. McClellan now hurled his army against the united force stationed on the old battlefield of Bull Run. The casualties on both sides in this crucial battle were horrific, but the Federal forces under General Pope were defeated, and had to retreat towards Washington. It was then feared that the capital would fall into the hands of the South.

In Britain, the pro-Confederate Prime Minister, Viscount Palmerston, saw this as a golden opportunity to move Britain's foreign policy towards favouring the South, as the following correspondence between Palmerston and Foreign Secretary Lord John Russell shows:

"94 PICCADILLY: September 14, 1862

"My dear Russell, The detailed accounts given in the *Observer* today of the battles of August 29 and 30 between the Confederates and the Federals show that the latter got a very complete smashing; and it seems not altogether unlikely that still greater disasters await them, and that even Washington or Baltimore may fall into the hands of the Confederates.

"If this should happen, would it not be time for us to consider whether in such a state of things England and France might not address the contending parties and recommend an arrangement upon the basis of separation?

"Yours sincerely, PALMERSTON"

"GOTHA: September 17, 1862"

"My dear Palmerston, Whether the Federal army is destroyed or not, it is clear that it is driven back to Washington and has made no progress in subduing the insurgent states. Such being the case, I agree with you that the time is come for offering mediation to the United States Government with a view to the recognition of the Confederates. I agree further, that, in case of failure, we ought ourselves to recognise the Southern State. For the purpose of taking so important a step, I think we must have a meeting of the Cabinet. The 23rd or 30th would suit me for the meeting.

"We ought then, if we agree on such a step, to propose it first to France, to Russia and other powers as a measure decided upon by us. We ought to make ourselves safe in Canada, not by sending more troops there, but by concentrating those we have in a few defensible posts before the winter sets in. I hope to get home on Sunday, but a letter sent to the Foreign Office is sure to reach me.

"(RUSSELL)"(9)

Whilst Palmerston and Russell made plans in London, progress continued to be made on the construction of the Confederate Rams in Laird's shipyard. Slidell was also highly active in France, obtaining an interview with the Emperor on 28 October, the objective of which was to advance his plans for the construction of Confederate warships in France. As French law on this issue was also something of a problem, he suggested to the Emperor that he would welcome some form of verbal assurance that his police would not observe too closely when he wanted to put arms and men on the ships!(10)

## A close encounter

The month of October 1862 had also been a particularly active one for Semmes on the *Alabama*. He managed to capture no fewer than eleven Federal ships, most of which he burned. November was less active, for he only took three ships: the whaler *Levi Starbuck*, an exceptionally valuable whaling vessel, which, with her cargo, was worth $203,962; and the even more valuable ship *Thomas B. Wales*, which was taken and burned on 8 November.

Semmes was by now running short of coal, an eventuality which had been carefully provided for. The *Alabama* was to meet her tender the *Agrippina*, which had shipped a cargo of coal for her at Cardiff, at St Pierre, Martinique. Captain McQueen arrived at the island ahead of Semmes on 11 November, and at once put the story around that he was acting upon instructions received from the local British consul, William Lawless. Needless to say Lawless took exception to this, and promptly took McQueen to task. Lawless made his way back to his base at Port Royal where, on the morning of 18th, a black, rakish-looking screw steamer was seen approaching the land, steering for Fort de France. As she passed before the town she showed a British Blue Ensign and Pennant, but this ploy failed to deceive anyone on the island, all recognising her instantly as the notorious Confederate raider *Alabama*.

The first thing Semmes did on arrival was to send a message to the Governor, asking permission to land 53 prisoners. This was agreed, all being landed and sent to the United States consul. Among the prisoners landed were the American consul at Mauritius and his family, who had been

*James M. Mason,*
*Confederate Commissioner*

returning to New York when the vessel conveying them had been captured by Semmes. The consul later informed Lawless that he had been treated very well whilst on board the raider, but this was in stark contrast to the treatment meted out to all other prisoners, officers and crew alike, who were kept in irons by Semmes. Lawless's report that the *Alabama* seemed to be well provided with fuel was incorrect, for her coaling arrangements had been disrupted, and it was only later that Semmes and McQueen were able to organise the transfer of the coals from one ship to another, at Blanquilla. While the prisoners of the *Alabama* were being taken ashore, McQueen and Semmes shook hands and parted, and within hours the *Agrippina* was heading out of port, having cleared for Demerara. Semmes then let it be known that he too would be leaving during the night, but those ashore noted that the *Alabama* was still at anchor on the morning of the 19th.(11)

Meanwhile the steamer *San Jacinto*, now commanded by Captain Ronckendorff, had been ordered to cruise in the West Indies in search of the *Alabama*. This was the vessel which, under the command of Captain Wilkes, had stopped the *Trent* and taken on board Messrs Mason and Slidell, the Confederate commissioners, causing the celebrated international incident.

It was at about 7am on 19 November, whilst the *Alabama* lay at anchor in Port Royal harbour, that the *San Jacinto* made her appearance. However, Ronckendorff refused to enter the harbour on learning that, under international law, he would then have to remain in port until 24 hours after the departure of his adversary. He was informed by a letter from the Governor that he must remain at a distance of three miles from the nearest land, and that any attempt to violate the neutrality of the port would be repressed by force of arms if necessary.

The Governor backed up his words with deeds, promptly ordering the forts to be manned and 24 rounds of ammunition to be allocated to each gun that was bearing seaward; the officers in charge of those at the mouth of the bay had strict instructions to open fire upon the American warship should she attempt to move into territorial waters. Shortly after these orders had been put into operation an obliging French warship which was in port was sent out, and took up a position between the rival ships.(13)

Meanwhile, the *Alabama* remained perfectly still, Semmes keeping his crew occupied in painting and repairing the masts and rigging. At first Raphael Semmes had taken the *San Jacinto* for another Federal vessel roughly equal to his own ship in firepower, and had therefore sent a message to the Governor to say that he intended to go out and engage her, but on establishing that she was in fact the *San Jacinto* rapidly reviewed his tactics.

The *San Jacinto* was actually a far more powerful vessel than the *Alabama*, having superior armaments, a more numerous crew, and in many other ways every advantage over the Confederate raider. Semmes decided therefore to make a run for it rather than fight, but at the same time, just in case he

had to do battle with Commander Ronckendorff, the guns were prepared and loaded; they were then run out and everything made ready for an encounter.

Shortly before sunset a small boat was seen leaving the harbour, heading in the direction of the *San Jacinto*. She was taking out one of the captains who had just been released by Semmes, and who had been sent by the United States consul to arrange for signals to be made from an American schooner anchored near the *Alabama*, in case the raider tried to make a run for it during the night.

Unfortunately for Ronckendorff, Semmes had spotted the boat leaving, put two and two together, and correctly guessed what was afoot. He promptly sent word to the captain of the port for a pilot, who came off without delay, and at dusk the raider started to move. At first he made for the inner port, but as soon as he was out of sight of the suspect schooner altered his course, so as to run out on the south side of the bay. The pilot had already left him half an hour when the master of the schooner, returning from the *San Jacinto*, found that the *Alabama* had left, and sent up three rockets in the direction which the crew told him she had taken. The *San Jacinto*, under full steam, ran to the south side of the bay, but not surprisingly failed to find the raider.

## John Ancrum Winslow

Semmes had escaped once more, but back in America interesting developments were taking place concerning the career of Captain John Ancrum Winslow, the man who would one day ensure that Semmes would not escape from an encounter with a Federal warship.

John Ancrum Winslow was an interesting character, whose attitude to slavery, the crucial issue of the day, was totally different from that of Raphael Semmes. The two men had messed together while serving on the USS *Cumberland* off Vera Cruz in the Mexican war, and by all accounts got on fairly well. In the course of these naval operations a small vessel had been captured, which was put under Winslow's command, and at about the same time Semmes was given the brig *Somers*. Winslow managed to pile his ship on a reef near Tampico, whilst Semmes was caught with all sails standing in a violent storm, losing his vessel as well. The two young lieutenants therefore found themselves transformed into division officers on the USS *Raritan*. The loss of their vessels became something of a standing joke between them at the time, but for men with such diametrically opposed outlooks this superficial bond was not something upon which a lasting friendship could be built.

On the question of slavery, Winslow held the same views as most of his co-religionists in New England. He was totally committed to the abolition of the system. The Civil War to Winslow was therefore more a *bona fide* crusade to take the yoke from the necks of millions of black men, than a war particularly dedicated to saving the Union. This, to him, was very much a secondary consideration.

Winslow's service in the old navy, except for fairly regular interruptions caused by ill health, was fairly typical. He was commissioned as a lieutenant in 1839, served at various times at sea and ashore, but on returning to Norfolk in 1855 he was promoted to commander and given shore duty that lasted for five years. When the Civil War broke out he was working as Inspector of the Second Lighthouse District, with headquarters in his beloved Boston. He at once applied for duty afloat.

Commander Winslow soon saw active service on the Mississippi, where he was given command of the ship *Baron de Kalb*. He then took temporary command of the flagship *Benton*, but whilst he was running between St Louis and Cairo she ran aground. Heavy hawsers were fastened to strategically located trees, and the steam winches linked up. Under the strain a chain broke, and flew wild, injuring his arm. This rendered him unfit for duty for several months, and he was invalided home. It was not until the following June that he was again ready for active service, when he returned to his command with the river flotilla. It was then that news got through about the Confederate gains in the east, and Bragg's excursion into Kentucky, all of which began to make Winslow openly critical of the entire conduct of the war in general and of Lincoln in particular. To the abolitionist Winslow the prime issue at stake was the elimination of slavery, and not the saving of the Union. News of some of his outspoken comments about Lincoln drifted back to Assistant Secretary Gustavus V. Fox, and Winslow had to admit that he had made some questionable comments about Lincoln.

After further incidents Captain Winslow reached his home in Roxbury, Massachusetts, early in November 1862. Four weeks passed before he heard from the navy that he was being given a new command, no doubt after some considerable consultation over where to assign a Federal captain who had admitted that he would be willing to see the Confederates 'bag old Abe' in order to wake up the Government! At last his orders arrived to take command of the *Kearsage*, a 1,031-ton steam sloop, which mounted seven guns. At the time he received these orders he was confined to bed, his doctor being of the opinion that he was so sick that he was not even fit to travel to his station, let alone take command of a ship. Amongst other things he suffered from an eye complaint, which might have been cured had he remained ashore; as it was, his acceptance of this command was to cost him the use of an eye. Nevertheless, he travelled all the way to New York, accompanied by his concerned son, and boarded the *Vanderbilt*, which was to take him out to his ship.

The *Vanderbilt*, which was to call at Fayal in the Azores, was also on a cruise in search of the Confederate raider *Alabama*. On Christmas Eve 1862, her Commander, Acting Lieutenant Baldwin, put Winslow ashore at Fayal, and then headed southwards in hot pursuit of Semmes. Winslow then had a long wait, for Captain Pickering, then the commander of the *Kearsage*, had put her into dry dock at Cadiz, just before receiving orders that he had a relief waiting for him at Fayal.

During this period Captain Winslow's physical condition grew steadily worse. The inflamed lungs, malaria, and serious eye condition which had kept him confined to his bed before he had set off for New York, continued to torment him. For six weeks he suffered, then seemed to improve a little until the day the *Kearsage* arrived, when his various ills returned with renewed vigour.

In this sorry condition the dedicated abolitionist Captain John Ancrum Winslow in the *Kearsage* began his long, and eventually successful, search for the dedicated supporter of slavery, Captain Raphael Semmes, in the Confederate raider *Alabama*. For the next few months Winslow cruised around the Azores, following one rumour after another regarding the possible location of the *Alabama*. He eventually realised that his presence was becoming so well known to the Confederates that they would, by now, be avoiding the area, and set sail for Cadiz.(13)

## The *Alabama*'s winter cruise

Meanwhile, during the winter months of 1862, the elusive Semmes continued to attack the defenceless ships of the United States merchant marine -although with far less success than had been the case in previous months. In December he 'scored' only two vessels, the schooner *Union* and the mail steamer *Ariel*. On 7 December Semmes came upon the Federal ship *Ariel*, which was then on passage from New York to Aspinwall. After a short chase, during which she sustained some damage from the guns of the *Alabama*, she was brought to.

The *Ariel* had on board 140 officers and men of the Federal marine, and some 500 other passengers. Although it might have made military, but not humanitarian sense, for Semmes to have arbitrarily destroyed this ship, he did not do so. Instead he treated all on board with great courtesy. Semmes was well aware that the eyes of the world were upon him and his ship, and that all he did was being noted by the international community. The oppressive regime that he represented was trying to gain international recognition and respectability as a legitimate state, and in such circumstances diplomatic considerations largely dictated his actions. Apart from the Federal marine and passengers, the ship was also carrying, as part of the cargo, one 24 pounder rifled cannon, 125 rifles, 16 swords, and 1000 rounds of ammununition. In three secure boxes the crew of the *Alabama* also found United States Treasury notes to the value of $261,000.00, which Semmes and his mercenary crew naturally stole. Two days later the *Ariel* was liberated, on her captain giving Semmes a ransom bond.

The *Alabama* spent the next few days cruising off the Western coast of Cuba before making for the three islands called Las Arcas, where the ship remained until 5 January 1863, undergoing repairs and taking supplies of coals and stores from her tender, the *Agrippina*. Before the departure of the vessel the steerage officers set up a graveboard on the most prominent point of the largest island, bearing the following inscription:

"In memory of Abraham Lincoln, President of the late United States, who died of nigger-on-the-brain, 1st January, 1863."

A note written in Spanish was also left in a protected and conspicuous position near the grave board:

"Will the finder kindly favour me by forwarding this tablet to the United States consul at the first port he touches at?"

After this performance the *Alabama* weighed anchor; Semmes resolved to take his ship and mercenary crew to the port of Galveston, Texas, then blockaded by Federal cruisers. The chances were that they would meet up with a Federal ship, and they prepared accordingly. They were not to be disappointed!(15)

## The Laird Rams

Meanwhile, back at Birkenhead, Messrs Laird & Company continued to work on the two Confederate ironclad rams. Bulloch was so pleased with the progress being made that he was able to inform Confederate Secretary of the Navy Mallory that one of these ships would be ready to put to sea by April 1863. He also outlined a devious plan of action, which included a rendezvous for ship and crew near the Azores which would not break England's neutrality laws and proclamations. To Mallory's thinking, however, this part of Bulloch's scheme was questionable, and he vetoed the whole plan.

The construction of the Laird Rams was by now making Palmerston and the British Government more and more restive. United

States consular spies in the hands of the astute American Minister, Charles Francis Adams, were doing their work well, and fears of an open conflict with America over the issue were mounting. James Dunwoody Bulloch read the signs of the times correctly, and acting ostensibly on behalf of the Pasha of Egypt he made a whitewash sale of the ships to a firm of merchants in Paris. This started the Laird Rams along a devious course of double dealing and backstairs diplomacy which was to end in a complete reversal of policy by Napoleon III, blocking the Confederates' plan to build Southern ironclads in France.(15)

# Lincoln's proclamation

At the close of 1862 more plans and policies were being rethought in Europe, whilst in the United States the attitudes of millions in the North was changing towards slavery. When Lincoln was inaugurated few people were deeply concerned about the fate of negro slaves, many miles away in the Deep South. But two years of bloody fighting was convincing ever-increasing numbers that the Union could not exist part slave and part free, as Lincoln had put it in his speech at Springfield in 1858: "It must be all one thing or all the other." Acting on his own authority, Lincoln had already declared all slaves within the Confederacy to be free men.

So far, the war had been fought mainly as one for the preservation of the Union, but Lincoln now estimated that the time was correct to openly declare that it was a war for Union and freedom. The astute President knew that Palmerston and his Conservative Government were only waiting for a pretext to acknowledge the independence of the South. If, however, the North now made it clear that this was a war for the abolition of slavery, he knew that the working people of England would not allow the independence of the Confederacy to be acknowledged by their reactionary rulers.

The time to make such a declaration was clearly after some victory gained by the Union army. When McClellan and Lee stood face to face at Antietam, Lincoln "vowed to God" that if Lee were defeated he would issue the proclamation. Lee was defeated, and on 22 September 1862 the proclamation came forth declaring that if the Confederate States did not return to their allegiance before 1 January 1863, "all persons held as slaves" within the Confederate lines "shall be then, thenceforce, and forever free". The states did not of course return to their allegiance, and on 1 January 1863 a second proclamation declared the slaves free. This proclamation was particularly important in its effect upon English public opinion. The opening paragraph stated:

"That on the 1st day of January, A.D. 1863, all persons held as slaves within any State or designated part of a State the people whereof shall then be in rebellion against the United States shall be then, thenceforward, and forever free; and the executive government of the United States, including the military and naval authority thereof, will recognise and maintain the freedom of such persons, or

of Southern cotton, spoke with a different voice. On 31 December they met in the Free Trade Hall in Manchester, and sent President Lincoln an address of total support. It concluded with these words:

"It is a mighty task, indeed, to reorganise the industry not only of four million of the coloured race, but of five millions of whites. Nevertheless, the vast progress you have made in the short space of twenty months fills us with hope that every stain on your freedom will shortly be removed, and that the erasure of that foul blot upon civilisation and Christianity – chattel slavery – during your Presidency will cause the name of Abraham Lincoln to be honoured and revered by posterity. We are certain that such a glorious consummation will cement Great Britain to the United States in close and enduring regards. Our interests, moreover, are identified with yours. We are truly one people, though locally separate. And if you have any ill-wishers here, be assured they are chiefly those who oppose liberty at home, and that they will be powerless to stir up quarrels between us, from the very day in which your country becomes, undeniably and without exception, the home of the free. Accept our high admiration of your firmness in upholding the proclamation of freedom."(16)

President Lincoln wasted no time in responding to the working men of Manchester, replying to them on 19 January 1863. Amongst the comments he made were these notable observations:

"Under the circumstances, I cannot but

any of them, in any efforts they may make for their actual freedom."

*The Times*, organ of the British ruling class and totally sympathetic to the Confederacy, characterised the Emancipation Proclamation as a very sad document. The rest of the Conservative press made similar observations, but the working men of Manchester, many of them victims of the Union blockade regard your decisive utterances upon the question as an instance of sublime Christian heroism which has not been surpassed in any age or in any country. It is indeed an energetic and reinspiring assurance of the inherent power of truth and of the ultimate and universal triumph of justice, humanity, and freedom. I do not doubt that the sentiments you have expressed will be sustained by your great nation; and, on the other hand, I have no hesitation in assuring you that they will excite admiration, esteem, and the most reciprocal feelings of friendship among the American people.''(17)

To President Jefferson Davis, Lincoln's Emancipation Proclamation was the most execrable measure recorded in the history of a guilty man. During January 1863 he spoke to the Confederate Congress about the development, encapsulating his thoughts on the matter in these words:

"We may leave it to the instincts of that common humanity which a beneficent Creator has implanted in the breasts of our fellowmen of all countries to pass judgement on a measure by which several millions of human beings of an inferior race, peaceful and contented labourers in their sphere, are doomed to extermination, while at the same time they are encouraged to a general assassination of their masters by the insidious recommendations 'to abstain from violence unless in necessary self-defense'.''(18)

However, even before the Emancipation Proclamation had been read, negroes were fighting Confederates. In 1862 the First South Carolina Volunteers had met and driven back an attack by Confederate soldiers and their bloodhounds. The main effect of Lincoln's Proclamation, however, was to open the United States armed forces to negroes, slave and free. Before the war ended 200,000 had entered the army and navy. One ship to benefit from this influx was the *Kearsage*.(19)

# CHAPTER 4

## 1863: THE *ALABAMA* CRUISE CONTINUES

January and February 1863 were eventful months in the Civil War, and this was reflected in the increased activity of the Confederate Raiders. Efforts were also made to increase the influence and strength of the South abroad, with corresponding efforts to oppose such developments by the North.

### The Confederates in France

Amongst those involved with the cause of the South was the Franco-British Erlanger Bank. In January 1863, the Confederate Congress floated a loan for 15 million dollars through this establishment which became known as the Erlanger Loan, and which was to be the only foreign loan effected by the Confederacy during the Civil War. Bonds were issued that would be convertible into certificates representing cotton in the Confederacy. Needless to say, the firm of Fraser, Trenholm & Company was entrusted with the management of all the cotton transactions, and the production of a prospectus for this huge loan.

For the Federal Government, the American Minister in London Charles Francis Adams started the year by noting the movements of Raphael Semmes' old ship – the *Sumter*. On 3 January he telegraphed the American consul at Gibraltar that Captain Bryson, commanding the United States war steamer *Chippewa*, was to endeavour to capture the *Sumter*, should she leave Gibraltar under the British flag; and on 19th he again telegraphed, "The *Sumter* should be captured, if she goes out of British waters on the high seas. If she has nominal British papers she must be sent home for adjudication as a prize." The American consul, on 21 January, answered as follows: "Your telegram communicated to our commanders: *Sumter* coaling again and provisioning to-day." She was to sail from Gibraltar on 7 February, and was not captured, reaching Liverpool on 13th. Here she remained until 3 July, all the time being watched by order of the British government as a precaution lest she should in any way be armed as a man-of-war again. When she sailed, however, she was carrying 'heavy ordnance' which the British officers merely noted could not have been used on the vessel itself, but which was, no doubt, of great value to the Confederacy. However, her continuing career in the service of the South was a short one, for she was subsequently wrecked attempting to enter the port of Galveston.(1)

Meanwhile in France, on 4 January, the day after Charles Francis Adams sent his telegram to the consul at Gibraltar, Mocquard, Napoleon's private secretary, informed Slidell that Napoleon had consulted some of his ministers and found greater obstacles than he had anticipated, and that for the present he could therefore not encourage the proposed Confederate shipbuilding project.(2)

However, three days later M. Arman – member of the Corps Legislatif, the largest shipbuilders in France, and in the confidence of Napoleon who consulted him on naval matters – came to Slidell and offered to build and arm ironclads for the Confederacy. He also confidently assured Slidell that there would no difficulties in arming and equipping such vessels. Not surprisingly Slidell felt sure that Arman came to him at the Emperor's suggestion.(3)

After more contradictory and intriguing developments Slidell was soon writing to Benjamin, stating that as soon as the success of Erlanger's loan was established he would write to Messrs Maury and Bulloch, suggesting that they came over to France for the purpose of ascertaining whether they could make satisfactory contracts. Slidell now sensed the need for some haste, as Bulloch was expressing grave doubts as to the probability of ever getting the Laird Rams, then nearing completion at Birkenhead, out of England. On this advice, and in accordance with his own opinion, Bulloch was soon to hasten to France to draw up draft contracts with Arman and T Vortuz Senior. Prudently, these contracts were drawn up under Slidell's condition that they should not be binding until the Emperor had clarified his position on the matter, and given his formal approval.(4)

# Two Confederate cruisers

However, two more Confederate cruisers did get to sea from English ports early in 1863: the *Rappahannock* and the *Georgia*. The former had a very short career. She was originally the Royal Navy dispatch vessel *Victor*, which the government found unserviceable and sold in November 1863 to a private individual, who happened to be acting for the Confederacy. After the sale she remained at Sheerness, refitting under the direction of persons connected with the Royal Dockyard. The Federal agents soon got wind of the development, and those concerned were alerted. Panic set in, and to escape detention she hastily put to sea – with the workmen still in her, and with only a part of her crew, which had been enlisted by the Inspector of Machinery at the dockyard. Despite these crude violations of the Foreign Enlistment Act, and Britain's supposed neutrality obligations, she was commissioned in the English Channel as a Confederate man-of-war.

Proceeding to Calais, her commander then had the audacity to claim admission to the port as his vessel was a ship-of-war in distress, and needing repairs. The impudence of this demand was too much even for the most sympathetic neutral; and after the commander had made some attempts to enlist more men and get his ship ready for active service, her operations were summarily ended by a French gunboat, which was stationed across her bow. Finding it impossible to fit her out, her commander finally had to abandon her.

By contrast, Confederate efforts in Scotland were crowned with success. Here the Clyde-built *Georgia*, a screw-steamer of about 600 tons, was launched in January 1863, putting to sea in April under the name of *Japan*. A Liverpool firm was employed as the intermediary to attend to all the transactions connected with the vessel. She was registered as a British vessel, and to provide further legal cover one member of this firm was her ostensible owner, whilst another took charge of a small steamer, the *Alar*. Following the pattern established by the *Alabama* and her tender the *Agrippina*, the *Alar* was then freighted with guns, ammunition and stores and met the *Japan* or *Georgia* at Morlaix, near Ushant off the French coast, where her preparations were completed.(5)

Although this vessel had left Greenock supposedly as an ordinary ship of commerce, her departure had been accelerated by a suspicion that the British authorities had received knowledge of the true nature of the vessel. In fact, orders to detain her reached Greenock the day after she had passed out of the Clyde. Command of the ship was given to W.L. Maury, the First Lieutenant being Chapman. Of the original seamen who had come out from Greenock and signed for a trading voyage, only 13 consented to sign as man-of-wars men, while the remainder went back to England on the *Alar*; the crew of the raider was then filled by men brought out in that vessel.(6) These men had been engaged and advances made by the Liverpool agents well before the *Georgia* had left the Clyde. Proceedings were afterwards instituted

against the guilty parties for these transactions under the Foreign Enlistment Act, and they were sentenced to pay a paltry fine of £50 per man – a penalty hardly likely to deter the pro-Confederate money-grubbers of Liverpool from committing violations of neutrality. In the meantime, the *Georgia* had escaped.(7)

This Confederate cruiser's field of operation was to be the Atlantic Ocean. This had already been swept by the *Alabama* and other Confederate raiders, so that only the gleanings were left for her; but in her short career she made prizes to the value of some $406,000. The first ship she took was the *Dictator*, which was burned on 25 April. She then ran across to Bahia, Brazil, where she coaled, and continued to the Cape of Good Hope, capturing on the way the celebrated Federal relief ship *George Griswold*, bound for Liverpool with food and supplies for the starving cotton operatives of Lancashire. To his credit, Maury did not follow the example set by Raphael Semmes when he destroyed the Federal relief ship *Brilliant*, for Maury merely bonded this relief vessel and allowed her to continue on her way to Liverpool.

After taking various other ships, the *Georgia* arrived at St Simon's Bay on 16 August, and on 29th set out for a return to Europe. During this run she made prizes of the *City of Bath*, *Prince of Wales*, *John Watts*, and *Bold Hunter*. She eventually arrived at Cherbourg, France in October 1863, when Maury left her on account of ill-health and Lieutenant Evans was promoted to commander. However, because of her insufficient sail power which necessitated frequent coaling, it was not deemed worthwhile to continue her as a cruiser, and she was taken to Liverpool where she was dismantled and offered for sale. Edward Bates, the well-known Liverpool merchant, became her new owner.(8)

## The *Georgiana*

In the record of ships built by Messrs Laird Brothers of Birkenhead there is no trace of one particular vessel, the fast and powerful Confederate steamer *Georgiana* – an interesting clerical oversight on the part of the builders of the *Alabama*.(9) This Laird-built 'Ghost Ship' escaped from British jurisdiction under the pretence of being destined for the Chinese naval service. This was a ploy the Laird brothers particularly favoured: for before launching the two 'Rams' -listed as Her Majesty's armour-clad vessels *Wivern* and *Scorpion* (which they did indeed become after being impounded by the Royal Navy) -they launched the screw-steamer *Tiensin* and the paddle-steamer *Kwang Tung*, both ostensibly built for the Chinese naval service. Unlike the *Georgiana* they were at least recorded in the Laird's list, but the *Kwang Tung* almost certainly became the Confederate blockade runner *Mary*.

The *Georgiana* left Liverpool bound for Nassau on 22 January 1863 with the intention of running the blockade into Charleston, where the ship was to be armed and fitted out as a cruiser. Why the Confederates chose such a risky procedure for fitting out this raider and not the others is not clear, but they paid the price for their foolhardiness.

After being detained for some time at Nassau she started for Charleston, but was spotted by Federal cruisers off the port; her commander opted for running her aground, about 20 March, on Long Island Beach on the South Carolina coast to avoid capture. Strenuous efforts were then made by the Federal navy to obtain her cargo, which was partly of military stores and known to be very valuable. The Confederates managed to keep off their landing parties by bringing field batteries to bear upon them, but unfortunately for the Confederates their ship was blown to pieces by their own shells. Apart from her cargo, the loss of this vessel was a serious one to the Confederacy, as the Laird family had built her as a much faster and stronger ship than any of the other Confederate raiders afloat, including the *Alabama*, and she would have made a superb man-of-war.(10)

## Federal setbacks

Meanwhile, thing were not going well for the Federal forces of Abraham Lincoln. On 13 December 1862 General Ambrose E. Burnside ordered the Army of the Potomac to do the impossible: to dislodge General Robert E. Lee's army from an almost impregnable ridge called Marye's Heights behind Fredericksburg.

At opposite ends of the battlefield, Union Generals Sumner and Hooker assaulted the heights no fewer than 14 times in their efforts to breach the Confederates' position. The stubborn bravery of the Union soldiers in the assaults was phenomenal. Even Lee, watching from his vantage point on the heights, was unable to believe the carnage resulting from Burnside's tactics. As night approached the Union army consolidated below the heights. Unbelievably, the following morning, Burnside ordered the attack to be continued, but only skirmishes occurred -for the men had lost heart, and eventually his more sober generals persuaded him that further action was futile. In this battle, hailed as a great victory for the Confederacy, Southern casualties were approximately 5,000 killed or wounded, as opposed to Union losses of more than 12,000. The results of the battle of Fredericksburg shocked Union sympathisers and badly damaged the morale of the Army of the Potomac. To put matters right Lincoln replaced Burnside with Major General Joseph Hooker, known as 'Fightin' Joe', in January 1863.

## Success for the *Alabama*

On the *Alabama* Raphael Semmes and his Confederate officers were being kept well advised of all developments in the conflict. Federal newspapers, without much regard for 'National Security', were allowed an astonishing latitude in dispensing news of the movements of armies and fleets, and the captured vessels frequently supplied Semmes, through copies of these newspapers, with information of great value, enabling him to avoid Federal cruisers and to learn of the movements of armies and transport ships destined to points of attack on the Southern coast. Information received

in this manner prompted Semmes to attempt the destruction of a Federal transport fleet led by General Banks and scheduled to land troops at Galveston, then in the possession of United States Forces with the intention of taking Texas. General Banks was expected off Galveston about 10 January 1863.(11)

Aware of all these plans in December 1862, Semmes set sail for the coast of Mexico, arriving off Cape Catoche on the night of 20 December. On the night of 22nd the *Alabama* dropped anchor in 20 fathoms of water, in the open sea. Getting under way the next morning she soon made out a barque, heading in the same direction as herself. This was her tender the *Agrippina* – both ships making for the nearby Arcas Islands, where they were scheduled to meet once more. The incorrigible Scots captain had taken all of four weeks to make his way from Blanquilla, having stopped on his way to 'refresh' his crew and do a little private trading. However, Semmes let him off with a gentle reprimand, and they ran in to the Arcas together, both ships anchoring alongside each other around 5pm. They remained here a week, coaling ship, refitting and painting.

On 5 January 1863 the *Alabama* left the islands and headed for Galveston, Semmes allowing himself five days in which to make the distance under sail. On 11th they were just 30 miles from Galveston. Semmes now laid his ship's head for the Galveston Lighthouse, and stood in expecting to get a distant sight of the Banks fleet before nightfall and then haul off and await the approach of night before making the assault.

The man at the mast-head of the *Alabama* had been told by Semmes to keep a sharp look-out for an immense fleet anchored off the lighthouse. The look-out at length cried out "Land ho! Sail ho!" Semmes, delighted at the prospect of taking a fleet of unarmed transports, eagerly questioned his look-out, who said he could not see any fleet of transports but only five steamers which looked like men-of-war. "Here was a damper!" Semmes was later to write, "What could have become of Banks, and his great expedition, and what was his squadron of steam ships-of-war doing here?"(12)

A few moments later a shell was seen to burst over the city – clearly thrown by one of the steamers. Rapidly putting two-and-two together, Semmes correctly deduced that the city of Galveston had been retaken by the Confederacy, as the United States Navy would not be shelling their own side. In fact the city had been taken back by the Confederate General Macruder, assisted by Captain Leon Smith of the merchant service.

The recapture of Galveston had changed the destination of the Banks' expedition. It rendezvoused at New Orleans, from which point General Banks later attempted to take Texas by way of the Red River valley. "What was to be done in this changed condition of affairs?" Semmes wrote later. Although he had promised his crew some 'sport', fighting five ships-of-war was clearly more than he had bargained for; but to go back on his word would have led to a loss of face, and rumblings that he was only willing to tackle defenceless ships of the merchant marine.(13)

It was while Semmes was trying to resolve the problem that his look-out called out again, informing him that one of the steamers had detached itself from the fleet and was heading directly for the *Alabama*. This vessel was the Federal gunboat *Hatteras*, which had spotted the *Alabama* and mistaken her for a merchantman running the blockade. Semmes decided to treat the vessel as a hunter baits a hog with corn to lure it from its lair, by lying to until the *Hatteras* approached, and then taking advantage of greater speed to get well ahead again. This game continued for several hours, until by about 8pm the gunboat had been taken some 25 miles away from the other ships in the Federal fleet. At this safe distance from the fleet Semmes waited for the *Hatteras* to catch up with him.

The *Hatteras*, under the command of Captain Blake, was not a custom- built man-of-war like the *Alabama* but a converted paddle wheel river steamer of some 1,200 tons, and a vessel of no great stability. Her armaments consisted of three rifled 68 pounders, four 32's smooth bores, one rifled 20 pounder, and a 12 pounder howitzer; and her crew of 17 officers and 102 men.(14)

In the darkness of the night the two ships approached each other very rapidly, then simultaneously stopped their engines when they were 100 yards apart. The *Hatteras* was the first to hail. "What ship is that?" "This is her Brittanic Majesty's steamer *Petrel*," the *Alabama* replied. The *Alabama* hailed in turn, but, according to Semmes, the reply was not very distinct, although they did make out the words "This is the United

States ship ----'', which was all the confirmation the Confederate vessel required. Presently the *Hatteras* hailed again, and said: "If you please I will send a boat on board of you." The *Alabama* indicated a willingness to receive the boarding party and within minutes the creaking of the tackle could be heard as the boat was lowered into the water. As the time left for further subterfuge had run out, Semmes decided that it was an opportune moment to play the role of an officer and gentleman, so that he could not later be accused of striking the *Hatteras* whilst sailing under false colours. However, to avoid being over-generous in his noble gestures, and run the risk of being involved in a fair fight, it was further agreed that the actual declaration of the Confederate ship's identity would also be the signal to open fire! Not a split second was to separate the two events. Kell now rang out "This is the Confederate States steamer *Alabama*!" and at the same instant gave the signal to fire.(15)

The last word had barely passed his lips when sky and water were lit up by the flash of the *Alabama*'s broadside, instantly followed by that of the Federal ship. About six broadsides were fired from the *Alabama*, but the action lasted for only about 13 minutes. The *Hatteras* then began to sink, and was obliged to surrender. The *Alabama* picked up the survivors, and steamed away at her best speed.(16)

*Captain Raphael Semmes, CSN*

This combat had made the locality of Galveston unpleasantly warm for the *Alabama* – several of the United States warships being instantly detached from the fleet to catch her. Semmes headed for Jamaica via the Yucatan passage and, having obtained permission from the Governor, anchored in Port Royal for repairs and coaling. The officers and crew seem to have received a great welcome here and enjoyed themselves enormously, to the extent that Semmes seemed to lose control of some of them for a while. A chief petty officer was put in irons for exceeding his time of leave. The paymaster was also dismissed from the ship for ''circumstances of a painful nature'', and sent ashore.(17)

The fact that the *Alabama* received such a welcome in the British colony of Jamaica is not to be wondered at, for many in such places were making a fortune from blockade running for the South. Some Englishmen also did not fully comprehend the underlying causes of the war, and their judgement of the South was flavoured by Confederate propaganda which presented the South as a weak and noble underdog struggling for independence and 'freedom'.

## Events in Europe

Meanwhile, in Europe on 11 January 1863, whilst the *Alabama* was busy sinking the *Hatteras*, Slidell was fighting a diplomatic struggle. The Confederate agent was doing his best to persuade the Emperor to allow the Confederates to built ships-of-war in France, but the Emperor, taking international relations into account, was less than enthusiastic about the proposition.

On Merseyside, James Dunwoody Bulloch was also becoming increasingly despondent about his chances of getting his latest creations, the Laird Rams, out of British waters for the Confederacy. He was now belatedly, and unsuccessfully, trying to transfer the ironclads to France to complete their equipment.(18)

## The *Florida* at sea

However, Confederate efforts to get the Merseyside-built raider *Florida* out of Mobile and into active service were successful. After her disastrous start, she was finally fitted out and manned at Mobile, and on the night of 15 January 1863 made her escape to sea. She was vainly pursued by the United States gunboat the *R.R. Cuyler* but managed to outrun this ship. With Lieutenant James Newland Maffitt in command, the raider then headed towards the west end of Cuba, where she arrived just a few days later. Here she managed to capture and burn her first prize, a small brig. Maffitt then put his ship into Havana, where she remained for 48 hours taking in coal, and on 25 January arrived at Nassau having taken two more prizes in the meantime, one of them the brig *Corris Ann*.

Admiral Wilkes, commander of the United States fleet in the West Indies, was now making all efforts to catch and destroy the *Florida*. Reasoning that as the *Florida* had just obtained coal at Nassau she would not, under the neutrality laws, be allowed to coal at another British port for three months, Wilkes concluded that she must go to the French island of Martinique for another supply of coal, and sent his ships off in that direction to look for her. In fact Maffitt had gone to the British colony of Barbados, where, upon his statement that his fuel had been exhausted by stress of weather, neutrality laws were once more overlooked by British officials, and he procured 90 tons of coal.

Cruising south the *Florida* halted at Green Cay to paint the ship, and the day after leaving the island the United States gunboat *Sonoma* was sighted. All hands were called to quarters, but the *Sonoma* failed to get close to the raider, and she continued on her cruise. Off the Windward Islands on 12 February she had a long chase with the celebrated American clipper-ship *Jacob Bell*, homeward bound from Foo Chow, China to New York. This magnificent clipper, with her cargo of silks and tea, was eventually caught and burned: she was later valued at $1,500,000, the most valuable single prize taken by any Confederate raider. After this catch the *Florida* continued her destructive cruise by heading towards Pernamboco, Brazil.(19)

## The *Alabama* escapes

On Monday 25 January, 5 days after arriving in Jamaica, the *Alabama* steamed out of the harbour at Port Royal at 8.30pm in an east-south-east direction, again escaping the attention of the United States warship *San Jacinto* and other Federal vessels watching for her outside the harbour. She kept on her course, bound for the coast of Brazil, and thence to the Cape of Good Hope. She was to make many captures of Federal vessels sailing between India, China, and Australia, and England and America, by masquerading as the Federal steamer *Dacotah* in seach of the Confederate pirate *Alabama*!

On the day after leaving Port Royal the watch on the *Alabama* spotted a ship which proved to be the barque *Golden Rule*, from New York, for Aspinwall. She was the property of the Atlantic & Pacific Steamship Comany, and was, with her cargo, worth $112,000. She was soon caught, and at about 6pm Semmes ordered the torch to be applied to the barque, noting later with some relish that the islands of Jamaica and St Domingo were both sufficiently near to witness the splendid bonfire which lit up the heavens far and near, soon after dark.

The next American ship to fall prey to Semmes was the *Chastelaine* of Boston, which had just left the island of Guadeloupe where she had been to deliver a load of staves, and was now on her way to Cienfuegos, Cuba, after a cargo of rum and sugar for her homeward passage. The crew were taken off, and then, a few moments later, the torch was applied, the sea walls of Alta Vela being lit by the unusual spectacle of a burning ship. Semmes took a particular delight in taking ships that hailed from this part of North America, where the people were notable for being the descendants of the Puritan founding fathers of the American state and still took an ideological lead from them on the issue of slavery.

Semmes then put into St Domingo to get rid of his prisoners. Given his attitude to the Puritan founders of the United States, and their opposition to slavery, his caustic comments on arriving at this place are revealing, and worth noting in full. "The old city of St. Domingo! How many recollections does it not call up! It was a large and flourishing city a hundred years before that pestiferous little craft, called the *Mayflower*, brought over the cockatrice's egg that hatched out the Puritan."(20)

It was at this time that Wilkes again exceeded his authority. The American Navy Department had sent out the *Vanderbilt*, one of the fastest steamers in the navy, on an independent mission to find and destroy the raider *Alabama*. Under the command of Captain Baldwin the *Vanderbilt*, showing remarkable foresight as to Semmes' likely movements, made her way towards the cruising ground of the Confederate raider, then near the equator.

This judicious plan was frustrated by Wilkes. On 28 February, the *Vanderbilt*, after looking in at Martinique and Guadaloupe, fell in with the USS *Wachusett* whilst off St Thomas. Admiral Wilkes came on board, decided he liked the vessel, and arbitrarily commandeered her for his own use! Having transferred his flag to the *Vanderbilt* he proceeded to Havana. He then had the audacity to write to the Department, informing them that he was very pleased with his new ship! Nothing would induce Wilkes to part with her until 13 June, when in obedience to strict and unambiguous orders from the Department, he allowed her to continue her cruise. But it was now too late: the bird had flown.(21)

# Pro-Union feeling in Britain

In Britain the distress in the North continued, where more and more mill operatives were reduced to a state of total destitution. Collections were now being made throughout the country. The Mansion House Committee held their weekly meeting on 23 January, at which it was established that the total raised had now reached £408,783, of which £294,145 had been remitted to the affected districts. In addition, the first cargo of goods which the people of the United States had voted to the Lancashire operatives arrived in the Mersey on 23 January. The cargo consisted of flour, and guano which was to be sold and the proceeds given to the distress fund. The American relief ship, *George Griswold*, with all sails set, was also outward bound from New York for Liverpool, with a large supply of provisions for the Lancashire operatives. Despite the pro-Confederate stance of Palmerston, this great clipper was to be welcomed on her arrival in the Mersey, in accordance with instructions from official quarters, by salutes from Her Majesty's ship *Majestic* and the batteries on each side of the river.

The workers of Great Britain continued to show their support for Abraham Lincoln, in contrast to the colonial powers in Jamaica who were so eager to help Semmes. As Lord

Charnwood later recorded, "When the largest manufacturing industry of England was brought near to famine by the blockade, the voice of the stricken working population was loudly and persistently uttered on the side of the North... it is a matter for pride, which in honesty should be here asserted, that with many selfish interests in this contest, of which they were keenly aware, Englishmen, in their capacity as a nation, acted with complete integrity."(22)

In January 1863 a great rally of Trade Unions was held in London in favour of the North. Henry Adams, writing to his brother, Charles Francis Adams, on January 27, informed him that they would not tolerate interference against us. He also assured his brother that this type of movement was as alarming to the British aristocracy as a slave insurrection would be to the plantation owners of the South. He concluded by stating that he never really appreciated the moral influence of American democracy, nor the cause that the privileged classes in Europe have to fear us.

Whilst Semmes and Maffitt cruised in the interests of the slave owners, feelings in the United Kingdom were indeed mounting against the South. On 7 February 1863 the press reported on the Emancipation Meeting held in Exeter Hall, London, when the huge crowd spoke out in favour of emancipation and the Union. Whilst one impassioned speech was being made there was suddenly a pause, and then, to great cheering, it was announced that the men of Bradford (4,000 strong) were at that very moment holding a similar meeting. It was proposed to send them a telegram saying, "We are for emancipation and the Union; what are you?" The same occurred one hour later with regards to Stroud, where an emancipation meeting was also being held. The abolitionist Taylor called John Brown the Garibaldi of America, and in doing so evoked a fitting honour to the man whose soul was, no doubt, marching on to the conquest of slavery. At the end of this meeting the reporters heard, to their amazement, that whilst they had been inside even larger meetings had been held outside. In all, four meetings had developed from this one intended meeting. The *Illustrated London News* could not refrain from commenting, "Whatever the result as regards North and South – the permanent rupture or the reunion of the States – it is impossible to doubt that the divine hand has so fashioned things as to destroy slavery."(23)

# CHAPTER 5

## LIVERPOOL SYMPATHY WITH LINCOLN

The town and port of Liverpool has a long and varied history, dating back to the reign of King John. The first dock was opened in 1720, and was followed by a series of bold engineering works designed to make the Rivers Mersey and Irwell navigable from Liverpool to Manchester, and the River Weaver from the Mersey to Nantwich, in the heart of the salt and cheese district. By the middle years of the eighteenth century Liverpool became the second seaport in Great Britain enjoying almost a monopoly trade of the Irish channel, with a huge maritime trade extending to the continent, America, the West Indies and Africa.

The cotton trade began from the east probably in the time of Queen Elizabeth, when the merchants from Turkey brought cotton wool from Cyprus to be worked on the Manchester looms. This trade was later to develop into a major industry, dependent on the importation of American cotton. The export of coal, iron, salt and crockery all featured in the development of the port, as did a major involvement in the whale trade.

The actual building of ships on Merseyside was also a major industry.

A more questionable kind of maritime adventure in which Liverpool was involved some 200 years ago was that of privateering against the commerce of the Americans and French. No fewer than 120 privateers were fitted out by Liverpool shipowners at that time. Looking back it seems amazing that the merchants of a civilised nation were allowed to steal their neighbours' goods at a time of war; nevertheless it happened. Firms which engaged in this trade operated under 'Letters of Marque', and their ships were allowed to fly their colours at the fore. Until the early years of this century the vessels of the Sandbache Tinne Company could be seen entering the Mersey with their flags flying in this position, while the vessels of the Brocklebank Line carried this tradition on until the middle years of this century.(1)

The trade conducted through the port of Liverpool was enormous, the best indication of this being the fact that by 1824 several thousands vessels were registered at the port. Between 1845 and 1853 the shipping of Liverpool doubled; the tonnage for the year ending 1853 amounted to nearly 1,000,000 tons.

The slave trade too was, until it was ended in 1807, a most lucrative branch of Liverpool enterprise. For many years most of the Liverpool business houses were, to a greater or lesser extent, involved in this trade. However, this became the subject of a stern and long-protracted controversy when Roscoe and other eminent citizens had the moral courage to denounce the unholy gains of their townsmen involved in the trade. It was a very different person, George Cook, the drunken tragedian, who once turned upon a Liverpool audience who had hissed him and fiercely exclaimed, "Every brick in your dirty town is cemented with a negro's blood!" Whilst this hysterical outburst from a third-rate drunken actor was never based on objective historical fact, it has been remembered to this day and is often quoted, serving as a harsh reminder of this sad period in Liverpool's history.(2)

From 1807, when the slave trade was abolished, Liverpool shipping became increasingly dependent on the movement of free Europeans to America and Australia, not slaves from Africa. Many of these emigrants themselves were the victims of poverty and oppression, particularly those from Ireland. Many intending emigrants never got further than Liverpool and were joined by thousands more, forced off the land by the industrial revolution, who came to Merseyside to seek work in the area. In this way the population of Liverpool had expanded and altered radically since the days of the slave trade. By the time of the American Civil War, Liverpool contained a population that was, in the main, as supportive to the abolitionist cause as any other town in the country. No fewer than seven Liverpool streets bear the name of the great abolitionist Roscoe, with the names of Rathbone, Wilberforce, Livingstone and Brougham being similarly honoured.

The involvement of many of Liverpool's merchants and shipbuilders with the Confederates in the middle years of the last century did, once more, link Liverpool with slavery. These elements also managed to attract a disruptive band of supporters. But two events, above all others, which took place in February 1863, emphasised the mass support Lincoln and the anti-slavery movement enjoyed in Liverpool at this time. One was the arrival of the United States relief ship *George Griswold*, and the other the great meeting held to show Liverpool's sympathy for Lincoln.

The American clipper-ship *George Griswold* was built at Quincey, Massachusetts, by Deacan Thomas, a man with a high reputation as a shipbuilder. She was a vessel of 1,280 tons, capable of carrying a cargo of 1,500 tons. Interestingly, because of the high price of cotton at this time this recently built clipper had sails made of Scotch hemp, rather than the traditional heavy cotton duck. However, sailing enthusiasts felt that this material did not hold the wind as well as the traditional material.

Despite the fact that the United States was in the midst of a bloody Civil War, and Lincoln's own troops were in desperate need of such supplies, the *George Griswold* was sent to Liverpool laden with food for the Lancashire operatives. Every duty or charge had been remitted in connection with this voyage on both sides of the Atlantic, and the commander, Captain Lunt and all his officers gave their services *gratis*.

The *George Griswold* set sail from New York for Liverpool on 13 January 1863. In her holds she carried 13,236 barrels of flour, pork, corn, rice, and various other supplies. She also carried over $30,000 in cash contributions for the distressed operatives. After an average run across the Atlantic she arrived at Liverpool on 9 February. As soon as she was off Port Lynas a telegraph was published, and a great reception put in hand; the New Steamtug Company immediately dispatched their powerful boat *Resolute* gratuitously to assist the ship into port.

The *Resolute* fell in with the ship at 3pm near the bar, and immediately took her in tow, but they did not reach anchorage in the river until nearly three hours after high tide. As she came up the river the clipper had the American and English flags flying, the tug also being well decorated for the occasion. On reaching the Rock Fort she was welcomed with a salute by lowering a flag, which was duly acknowledged, and shortly after entering the river the huge guns of the North Battery roared out an 18 gun salvo. Thousands lined the banks of the Mersey to ensure that this ship, her officers and crew, received the welcome they deserved. Shortly after her arrival the Liverpool Chamber of Commerce also presented an address to the officers of the *George Griswold*. The presentation took place at St George's Hall before a crowded and enthusiastic audience. The Central Relief Committee then organised a similar compliment to Captain Lunt and his officers.(3)

The great meeting at which Liverpool expressed sympathy with President Lincoln was held in the Royal Amphitheatre on 19 February 1863 – the culmination of many meetings, lectures and discussions that had

*President Abraham Lincoln*

been held in the town during January and February to show support for Lincoln. This meeting had been convened with a view to adopting an address to President Lincoln, "expressive of sympathy in the emancipation measures of his government, and in condemnation of the attempt to found a polity on the basis of negro slavery".

Between 3,000 and 4,000 people assembled, and every class of the community was represented. The chair was taken by John Cropper, and amongst those present was the Reverend C.W. Denison, chaplain of the *George Griswold*. In his long opening address Cropper brought the attention of the meeting to the notorious 'Cornerstone' speech of Stephens, Vice-President of the Confederate States, in which he had vowed to found a state based on slavery – "its foundation is laid, its corner stone rests, upon the great truth that the negro is not equal to the white man – that slavery is his natural and normal condition. Thus our new Government is the first in the history of the world based upon this truth. This stone that was rejected by the first builders, has become chief corner-stone of our new edifice." Cropper also drew the attention of the audience to revealing utterances of Jefferson Davis, President of the Confederacy. Though Davis had declined to vote in the State of Mississippi for the re-opening of the slave trade, he had covered himself carefully and said, "I have no coincidence of opinion with those who prate of the inhumanity of the slave trade." Finally Cropper quoted Stephens again, in a speech of 1857: "It is plain that unless the number

of the African stock be increased we have not the population and might as well abandon the race with our brethren of the North in the colonisation of the territories." Having established that the Confederacy's avowed aim was not only to perpetuate the slave system, but extend it into the new territories, the Chairman said he could not understand the feelings of those Englishmen and Christians who sympathised with it, or who expected that slavery would voluntarily be terminated.

When asked what President Lincoln had done to win their approval, the Chairman stated that it was more than any other President had done: his Government had enforced the law against slave trading; entered into slave trade treaties with Great Britain, conceding the right of search; prohibited slavery in the territories; abolished slavery in the district of Columbia; entered into diplomatic relations with the negro states of Hayti and Liberia; offered terms of compensated abolition to the loyal states; and finally, proclaimed liberty to the slaves in the rebel states.

Resolution after resolution was put to the meeting. Amidst roars of approval, the Reverend C.M. Birrell put one which said: "That in the opinion of this meeting the war now raging in the United States of America originated in the institution of slavery and in the antagonism which that system inevitably presents to the institution of freedom." After this resolution was debated another Minister, the Reverend J. Jones of Christ Church, proposed a resolution which read: "That in the emancipation policy the Federal Government is entitled to the generous sympathy of every Englishman, and to the moral support that such sympathy always affords.'' Speaker after speaker praised the Federal Government and condemned the Confederacy, until the immortal words of the noted abolitionist, Lord Henry Peter Brougham & Vaux, were read out to the thousands present:

''Talk not of the property of the planter in his slaves. I deny the right; I acknowledge not the property. The principle, the feelings of our common nature rise in rebellion against it. Be the appeal made to the understanding or to the heart, the sentence is the same that rejects it. In vain you tell me of laws that sanction such a claim. There is a law above all the enactments of human codes – the same throughout the world – the same in all time . . . It is the law written by the finger of God on the heart of man; and by that law, unchangeable and eternal, while men despise fraud and loath rapine and abhor blood, they will reject with indignation the wild and guilty phantasy that man can hold property in man.''

The meeting continued, with pro-Confederacy elements who had infiltrated the gathering doing what they could to disrupt the proceedings. When it was pointed out that Abraham Lincoln's policy had always been anti-slavery, and that his recent emancipation proclamation was the crowning act of a very worthy life, there was renewed cheering from the crowd – and further interruptions from Confederacy elements. When the Reverend Hugh Stowell Brown read out the advertisement convening the meeting, which had been called to adopt an address of support for President Lincoln, this was carried, and the meeting closed.(4)

## Shipbuilding continues

Whilst feelings of support mounted for Abraham Lincoln and the Federal Government on Merseyside, Messrs Laird & Company in Birkenhead and Miller & Company in Liverpool continued to complete orders for the Confederacy. Work on the Laird Rams was now well advanced, and Miller & Company were about to launch yet another blockade runner, the *Phantom*. Thomas H. Dudley, United States consul at Liverpool, noted all these developments and kept Charles Francis Adams well advised about the situation, writing to him following the launch of the *Phantom*:

''United States Consulate, Liverpool, March 24, 1863

''Sir: On Saturday last Mr William C. Miller & Son launched from their yard, in Liverpool, an iron screw-steamer, called the *Phantom*, built for Fraser, Trenholm & Co. This vessel is large and to have great speed. The contract is not less than seventeen nautical miles per hour. Her engines are being made by Fawcett, Preston & Co. She has three port-holes on each side. Captain Bulloch, Captain Tessier, Mr Prioleau, the leading members of the firm of Fraser, Trenholm & Co., Mr Thomas, of the firm of Fawcett, Preston & Co., and others were present at the launch. She is intended for the South, either as a privateer or blockade-runner; there is no doubt about this, I think. She will turn up a privateer. Her draught of water will be light, and with her powerful engines her speed will be very fast. When afloat she will be a most dangerous craft to our commerce, if armed with two or three guns.

"I have on several occasions referred to the steamer built at Stockton for Fraser, Trenholm & Co., called the *Southerner*. This vessel came here yesterday either to coal or else fit out as a privateer. There is no doubt about this vessel. I suppose it will be impossible for me to obtain legal evidence against these two vessels, and nothing short of this will satisfy this Government.

"Thomas H. Dudley"(5)

It seems clear that had the British Conservative Goverment under Palmerston wished to block this pro-Confederacy activity, they were well placed to do so, but that they chose not to – despite the ever-mounting

*19 Abercromby Square, Liverpool, residence of C.K. Prioleau of Fraser, Trenholm & Co in the 1860s. (Chris Sarson)*

concern of the British people about the true nature of the Confederacy.

The standard voyage of all these blockade-running vessels was to load arms, ammunition, general merchandise, coal and machinery at British ports, and clear for Bermuda, the Bahamas, Havana, or Halifax, where they would refuel, or take on additional cargo to refill the abnormal bunker space used for the outward voyage from England. Once fully loaded, and under cover of night, these vessels would then make a dash for Savannah, Wilmington, or other blockaded ports, where the cargo would be unloaded and replaced by cotton for export to Europe. This had to be done beneath the noses of the Federal warships which watched British colonial coasts, and of the ships actually blockading the Southern harbours.(6)

The work obviously required much courage, and the 'adventure' element in these trips no doubt attracted many youngsters to this service. Others were doubtless attracted by the prospects of high pay. The shipbuilders and merchants were clearly in the game for cash, regardless of ethics.

Following the mass pro-Lincoln meeting in Liverpool in February, local press reports about the activity of John Laird in Birkenhead and Semmes cruising in the Laird-built *Alabama* became noticeably more critical. One such report in March noted that everybody knew, and so did Mr Laird, that the *Alabama* was specially built for the Confederate Government, and intended to prey upon the property of the merchants of New York, Boston, and other cities in the Union. So far as Semmes and the *Alabama* where concerned it was noted that, whilst they were told she was a vessel of war, Semmes ran no risks. He avoided confrontation with his equals; he 'skedaddled' from any enemy capable of grappling with him, and put himself in friendly ports where he was inaccessible to his opponents. He would then steal out in the darkness of the night, or under the friendly connivance of authorities violating neutrality. There was no fight in him; and whilst they did not wish to accuse him of cowardice, his acts would justify the charge. He approached no blockade port, and aided no friendly vessel carrying supplies to his Government.

In the same report it was also noted from John Laird's speech, made in the House on the previous Friday, that he had been solicited to build one or more privateers for the Federal Government. The reporter felt it more than likely that he had been misled: the application had not come direct from the American Government, and may only have been testing his disposition to accept an order from a belligerent. Whilst Laird may have had grounds for concealing the gentleman's name, the reporter suggested that his grounds for this stand were insufficient; either the man was authorised to make the proposal or was not. If he were not he ought to be exposed; but if he were, no possible harm could come to him for having forwarded the business. Secrecy in political matters, the reporter stated, "always wears a hue of suspicion" and the nation was curious to obtain Mr Laird's secret!(7)

## Semmes continues his cruise

While the political arguments about the Confederacy and the Confederate raiders mounted, Semmes continued his cruise in the *Alabama*. On 23 March he made two more captures, the *Morning Star* of Boston, bound from Calcutta for London, and the *Kingfisher* of Fairhaven, Massachusetts. The former vessel was ransom-bonded, the latter Semmes burned. The following day the *Alabama* crossed the equator and on 25 March made two more captures. The voyage of destruction continued in a similar manner until they reached Bahia on 11 May. Here the ship was enthusiastically received, much to the concern of the authorities who were afraid of giving offence to the Federals. The American consul did in fact demand the seizure of the raider, but the request was not complied with. Semmes at once commenced coaling, received supplies, and put on shore a large number of prisoners taken from captured vessels.(8)

In this port Semmes and his crew were surprised to find themselves in the company of another Confederate raider, the *Georgia*, which was under the command of Captain W.L. Maury.(9) The crews of both Confederate ships then learnt that the *Florida* was at Pernambuco. This news made them feel able to boast of the "Confederate squadron of the South American Station". The *Florida* was actually having a very busy time cruising off· the coast of Brazil and taking many prizes. It was near here that Maffitt made a tender of the brig *Clarence* before working his way back to St George,

Bermuda, where he arrived on 16 July 1863. He had destroyed 14 prizes and bonded three.

The *Alabama* took her departure from Bahia on 21 May and steered for the Cape of Good Hope, committing the usual ravages on Federal merchantmen on the way. Amongst others, the *Talisman* was captured – a very useful catch as her cargo consisted of coals and she had on board two brass rifled 12 pounders. These guns, with a supply of small-arms, coals and stores were put on board another prize, the *Conrad*, which was turned into the Confederate cruiser *Tuscaloosa*.

Lieutenant John Low was given command of this new acquisition. Born in Liverpool, Low had been educated in the British Mercantile Marine but at the advent of the Civil War he had been living in Savannah. Putting himself at the service of the Confederacy, Low's undoubted abilities soon attracted the attention of James Dunwoody Bulloch, and he was accordingly appointed 2nd Officer of the *Fingal*. This vessel had then been loaded with war material, and, in company with Bulloch, Low had run the blockade into Savannah.(10) Once the new raider had been fitted out the two ships parted company. Captain Baldwin was now on the track of the *Alabama* in the USS *Vanderbilt*. Touching at the Brazilian ports, Baldwin found himself always on the enemy's tail, but a month behind her.

The *Alabama* eventually made land in the lattter part of July. Sails clewed up, they proceeded under steam to the anchorage of

Saldanha Bay, a British possession 60 miles from Capetown. In this safe and beautiful harbour, the crew of the *Alabama* enjoyed themselves hunting wild game, whilst the paymaster Galt concentrated on obtaining fresh supplies of beef, mutton, and fish. In the meantime Raphael Semmes communicated with the Governor of Cape Town advising him of the arrival of the *Alabama* in British waters and requesting, as customary, the hospitality of the colony. Lieutenant Sinclair, one of the ship's officers, felt that this was merely a matter of ceremony, for they had already experienced the hospitality of 'John Bull' – and knew they could depend on it!

Whilst most of the crew enjoyed themselves at Saldanha Bay and Semmes planned his grand arrival at Cape Town, Kell, the ever-active Executive Officer, was working hard to put the ship in good order, assisted by the Boatswain Mecaskey, Gunner Cuddy, Sailmaker Alcott, and Carpenter Robinson. After much effort she was at last repaired, and ready to make the short cruise to Cape Town. Semmes and his officers paid their respects to the Governor of the colony, Sir Philip Wodehouse, who had already given them an assurance of a great welcome at the Cape.(11)

The reception given to the Confederates at the Cape was even more cordial than they had experienced at Bahia. Private individuals and officials vied with each other in welcoming Semmes and his motley crew. Interestingly, the Confederate ship *Georgia* had just been in Simon's Bay but had departed for, it was thought, the Indian Ocean. She had only been gone a few days when the Federal cruiser *Vanderbilt* steamed in, hot on the trail of the Confederate pirates; on learning how short a time had elapsed since the *Georgia* left, she set off in pursuit. Had she been a few days earlier, or waited a few days longer, she would have been certain of encountering one of the Confederates – the *Georgia* or the *Alabama*.

*Master's Mate Max Von Meuinier, of The Alabama*

Whilst at the Cape two new officers joined the *Alabama*, both aristocrats and officers in the Prussian Navy, on leave of absence at the time. These were no less than Baron Maximilian Von Meulnier and his companion, Julius Schroeder, who were both engaged by Semmes as master's mates. The Baron and Schroeder were found to be excellent officers, the former being particularly useful to Semmes as he was familiar with many languages. His position in Prussian society, where the peasants were regarded as little more than slaves, probably disposed Von Meulnier towards strong sympathy for the Southern cause.(12)

Despite gaining the services of these two aristocrats whilst at the Cape, Semmes also lost 20 of his best men. He managed to fill their places by stealth, since the shipping offices were not open to him, and the neutrality laws did not permit him to ship them openly. Having obtained the men he required secretly, and aware that his actions were probably being monitored by the American consul, Semmes decided to make a run for it whilst the going was good. Anxious to avoid the law, Semmes was also even more anxious to avoid a fight with the *Vanderbilt* – then waiting for the confederate raider just off the Cape.

The eventual departure of the *Alabama* from Simon's Town was taken at night – to avoid the *Vanderbilt* – and in the teeth of a gale. The wind shrieked through the bare poles of the raider, whilst thunder and lighting, moonlight and cloud, added to the drama of the scene, as the *Alabama* headed for her next area of operation. Ships seen under such conditions in these latitudes no doubt did much to perpetuate the strange legend of the *Flying Dutchman*.

Once the raider was well clear of the Cape the propeller was hoisted, the fires banked, and she began to follow the way laid out by Captain Matthew F. Maury, previously of the United States Navy and Superintendent of the Naval Observatory at Washington, but now of the Confederate Navy. Maury's sailing directions bid them to 'run the easting down', passing by the barren isle of St Paul in the Southern Indian Ocean, as Semmes was now heading for the Straits of Sunda having decided to make the Far East his new hunting ground.

For the next six months the *Alabama* kept busy sweeping the seas in this part of the world of the Federal flag. And, like the *Flying Dutchman*, the *Alabama* was, over and over again, asserted to be in places at times quite irreconcilable with ordinary or even extraordinary sailing speed. She was at almost one and the same time reported to be in the West Indies Seas, doubling Cape Horn, cruising off the coast of California, and watching for Federal ships at Singapore.(13)

## The Battle of Gettysburg

In America during the summer of 1863, events were at last moving in favour of Abraham Lincoln and the Federal Government, all of which were soon to have repercussions in the Laird shipyard at Birkenhead. The Battle of Gettysburg began on the first day of July, with General Robert E. Lee aiming to strike a decisive blow for the Confederacy.

About midday he opened a terrific cannonade on the Federal lines and after an hour and a half ordered a charge of Pickett's brigade upon the centre of the Union line, which was under the command of General Hancock. The grey column swept across the open plain for a mile, while cannon and musket poured against them. Lee, seeing the hopelessness of trying to break the Union lines, now fell back and retreated across the Potomac.(14)

On 4 July, Lincoln announced the result of the battle to the people of the United States, saying that the army of the Potomac had been covered with the highest honour. That evening he was visited by a huge crowd of excited people, as the band played patriotic airs under the White House windows. After a while the President appeared at one of the central windows, and then, after a dramatic pause, he made his great congratulatory address to the vast crowd. All fell silent as he said: "I do most sincerely thank God for the occasion of this call." Then, reminding the people that it was the anniversary of the Declaration of Independence, and recalling the immortal words of the declaration to which he was dedicated, he said: "How long is it? Eighty odd years since, on the Fourth of July, for the first time in the history of the world, a nation, by its representatives assembled, and declared as a self-evident truth, that all men are created equal. That was the birthday of the United States of America." After making mention of some events of national importance related to Independence Day, he added: "And now at this last Fourth of July just passed we have a gigantic rebellion, at the bottom of which is an effort to overthrow the principle that all men are created equal." A few days later, Lincoln proclaimed a day of national thanksgiving, and thanked God for the victories of the United States army and navy in their efforts to preserve the Union and defeat American slavery.(15)

Negro troops, those recently emancipated from slavery, were now part of the Union forces. The standards for admitting them to the army were very high, and within months of their admittance they gained a reputation for bravery and exemplary service. As General Ullman was to remark, "They are far more earnest that we... They know the deep stake they have in the issue...".(16)

In Britain Palmerston and his Conservative Government were equally aware of the deep stake they had in the issue, losing no time in appreciating the significance of these latest developments in America. 'Old Pam' was wily enough to understand that the days of the Confederacy were now numbered, and that events would soon oblige him to stop flirting with it and establish a better relationship with the Federal Government. In this changed political climate, matters relating to the recently launched Laird Rams, now fitting out at Birkenhead, continued to occupy the attention of Dudley, the American consul in Liverpool, Adams in London, and indeed, Lincoln in America.(17)

# CHAPTER 6

## THE LAIRD RAMS

### The Laird-Bulloch contracts

Captain James Dunwoody Bulloch had arrived back in Liverpool in March 1862, with authority from his Confederate masters to organise the construction of two powerful ironclad ships-of-war. Precise details of the vessels were left to Bulloch's discretion. He opted for the turret type, rather than the conventional frigate type of armoured vessel. The concept was then discussed with the Laird Brothers, who gave their enthusiastic support. Needless to say, funding for this major shipbuilding project was to be drawn from Fraser, Trenholm & Company, Liverpool-based bankers to the Confederacy.

After long and careful negotiations it was finally agreed that Laird & Company would build two ironclad turret rams for a price of £93,750 each, to be delivered in April 1863. To circumvent British neutrality obligations and the terms of the Foreign Enlistment Act Bulloch was careful to make no formal mention of the Confederate Government, and the contract was drawn up in his name. Ostensibly the deal was presented as a normal commercial one between a shipbuilder and a private merchant. Apparently, the Laird brothers asked no awkward questions about the heavy armour plating, gun turrets or bow-rams, all of which were most unusual additions for a private individual's merchant ships.

Bulloch 'supposed' that the Laird brothers knew of his connection with the Confederacy, but at no time, he later insisted, did either side admit that they were building these ships for the Confederacy. Hiding behind this legal facade the Laird family felt that they could swear, in any subsequent enquiry, that as far as they knew the two rams were not for use against a power with which Britain was at peace. They had merely built two ships, to the order of a private individual who could later decide how they were to be used. The contract itself must have been a unique one, for in the annals of maritime history it is difficult to recall another instance when a 'private individual' has placed an order with a shipbuilder for two substantial men-of-war for his own personal use! Before signing this contract Bulloch did, however, consult his lawyers, wishing to ascertain from them whether armour plating could be construed as 'equipment' under the Foreign Enlistment Act; he was assured that the Act did not forbid the construction of any type of ship.

Interestingly, Section 7 of this Act did prohibit "any person in British Territory (without royal licence) from equipping, furnishing, fitting out, arming (or attempting or assisting to do so) any vessel with the intent that such vessel should be used to commit hostilities against any state with which this country was at peace". As the built-in projecting bow-rams on these ships could clearly have been classified as armaments, it is interesting to note that they were not. The term "equipping" was also open to interpretation, for the Oxford Dictionary definition of this word, as applied to ships, merely means to "furnish with requisites, provide for journey etc". The conveniently narrow interpretation put on this word in 1863 relating to this Act was that "equipping" a ship for war meant specifically putting guns and ammunition on the vessel as part of the initial contract. Avoid this by shipping arms out on a separate vessel, and all concerned would be in the clear. It was this interpretation of the law, as upheld by the British Government, that made the Laird-Bulloch contracts viable. British neutrality obligations were also bent in a similar manner to facilitate deals with the Confederates. Despite the shortcomings in the law and its interpretation, Charles Francis Adams, American Minister in London, constantly raised the issue with the Palmerston administration – objecting in principal to all that was being allowed.

Unlike the ship *Georgiana* built for the Confederacy, which does not appear on the list of ships built by Laird Brothers of Birkenhead, the two 'Rams' do. Vessels number 294 and 295 are, however, not listed as the *El Tousson* and *El Monassir*, under which names they were launched, but as Her Majesty's armour-clad turrets, *Scorpion* and *Wivern*. (These were the names later given to the vessels, after they had been impounded by the government under a compulsory purchase order.)(1)

The two 'Rams' were as well designed for swiftness as they were for strength. The length of each vessel was 230 feet, the beam 42 feet, and the draught when loaded about 15 feet. The deck was designed to be just 6 feet above the waterline. (This was a factor which was to tell against the vessels, when they were later placed at the disposal of the Royal Navy.) All the exposed areas of the ship's sides were protected with a coating of teak over the iron skin of the ship, and then by armour plate over that, each massive scale being 5.5 inches thick. The decks were also of 5-inch teak, covered with iron. Two revolving cylindrical turrets, on the well-known designs perfected by Captain Cowper Coles (relative of the Laird family, and designer of the ill-fated warship *Captain*) were apportioned to each ship, each turret carrying two guns placed in close proximity, so that they could be brought to bear in nearly the same position at one time.

The vessels took their name of 'Rams' from their most distinguishing feature, the massive metal ram which protruded about 7 feet beyond the prow. The idea was that the ship would run straight at the side of an enemy ship, driving the great ram into the adversary below its protective plate. This tactic had first been used in galleys, powered by rows of slaves manning huge oars. With the introduction of steam-power in the last century the concept was revived, and pursued with enthusiasm by naval architects in the 1860s. The Confederates intended to use these ships to attack the many wooden Federal vessels maintaining a close blockade on Southern ports, against which they would

*The Laird family Shipyard, 1860. (Williamson Art Gallery & Museum, Birkenhead)*

have been highly dangerous. The harbours of the South were also very shallow, a factor which the Laird brothers took into account when designing the vessels.

Work on the 'Rams' had started in the summer of 1862, Bulloch's early reports being optimistic about the progress being made on the contract. However, by the close of the year a more cautious note began to creep in. As is so often the case with large shipbuilding contracts, it was becoming clear to all concerned that the ships would not be completed on time. It was also becoming clear to James Dunwoody Bulloch that the United States consul in Liverpool, and Charles Francis Adams, the American Minister in London, were taking a great deal of interest in developments at Birkenhead.

On 11 July 1863 Adams took up the matter once more with Earl Russell, the Foreign Secretary. In a long note he complained about the pro-Confederate stance of the British Government, but also enclosed a letter from Dudley and four depositions, all intending to show what acts of hostility against the United States were taking place on Merseyside. Adams regarded the Confederate base at Liverpool as part and parcel of a plan of systematic warfare against the States, and noted with regret that in these efforts the Confederates had received the aid and effective co-operation of numbers of Her Majesty's subjects. The result had been the dispatch of a number of steam-vessels laden with arms and munitions. Adams then came to the question of the Laird Rams. Here he objected to the construction of steam vessels of war "of the most formidable kind" in the port of Liverpool, which were clearly being made for the Confederates. He regarded the work in progress at the Laird yard as being tantamount to a participation in the war by the people of Great Britain to a degree which, if not prevented, could endanger the peace and welfare of both countries.(2)

Adams was clearly indicating that the release of the Laird 'Rams' could lead to war between the United States and Great Britain. His thinly veiled threat came just one week after the Confederacy had been defeated conclusively at the Battle of Gettysburg. He had no doubt concluded that Palmerston and Russell would now have had time to reflect on the reality of the political and military situation in America, and would realise that the days of the Confederacy (and their supporters!) were now numbered.

## The French connection

However, even prior to Gettysburg, Bulloch had begun to worry about a change in British policy, and the possibility of the 'Rams' being detained by the British Government. He commented on the fact that the customs officers at Liverpool had been ordered to report on all armoured vessels that were under construction, other than for the Royal Navy. It was then that he hit upon the idea of (ostensibly) transferring the ownership of the ships to a foreign merchant.

Fitting in neatly with this ploy was the fact that Slidell, the Confederate agent working in France, had just made contact with a French Company based at Paris, Messrs Bravary & Company. This somewhat questionable organisation had a representative in Egypt, who, so Bravary maintained, had conveniently recently received a tentative enquiry from the Pasha of Egypt to build two men-of-war, with bow rams. There was good reason not to take as gospel all that Bravary said, for the firm was not the most reputable in Paris; a member of the firm had been accused on one occasion of keeping a brothel, taken the matter to court, but lost the case! However, the firm was noted for being willing to undertake risky and questionable contracts without asking too many questions. The required transfer documents were drawn up, and in this manner the Laird

'Rams' obtained the names *El Tousson* and *El Monassir*. Bulloch, as might be expected, had given much care and attention to the transfer documents, so that Confederate links would not show in any formal contract if the issue ended up in court.

## The evidence mounts

Other evidence was soon to be offered conclusively proving Confederate links with the Rams. In a long sworn statement made at the Custom House, Liverpool on 6 April 1863, Clarence R. Yonge, ex-paymaster on board the *Alabama*, gave much interesting evidence against Bulloch and on Confederate activity at Liverpool. He stated that he had come over to Liverpool with Bulloch, serving initially as his clerk. He had written many letters for Bulloch to sign, and from this correspondence he was well aware that Bulloch was a Confederate agent, and was responsible for the construction of the Miller-built *Florida*, and the Laird-built *Alabama*. So far as the Laird Rams were concerned, Yonge had learnt from his work conducted in the offices of Fraser, Trenholm & Company that Lieutenant James H. North had been sent over to England by the Confederacy to make contracts in England for the building and fitting out of iron-clad vessels, to make war upon the government and people of the United States. Bulloch had been directed by Mallory, the Secretary of the Confederate Navy, to assist North in making and placing these contracts.

Yonge further stated that he had visited the Laird shipyard when the *Alabama* was under construction, and had seen Bulloch and the Lairds together discussing the contract. He had also seen the Lairds at the office of Fraser, Trenholm & Company, where the Confederate flag was openly on display. Before he had sailed in the *Alabama* he had seen the plans, specifications and drawings made and furnished by William and John Laird for building the iron-clad Rams for the Confederate States. Yonge concluded his significant declaration:

''On the 5th day of April, 1863, I went to the shipyard of William and John Laird & Co., at Birkenhead. In the southerly part of the yard, under the shed, side by side, I saw two iron-clad ram steamers which they were building there. I believe them to be the same that I saw on the plans and drawings made by the Messrs Laird, and in possession of Captain Bulloch, at the office of Fraser, Trenholm & Co. hereinbefore mentioned. I had not the least doubt about the matter.'' (C.R. Yonge, 6 April, 1863)(3)

On 29 June George Temple Chapman made another deposition, in which he stated that he had called at the offices of Fraser, Trenholm and had spoken to Bulloch whilst there. Bulloch had referred to the *Alabama* and *Florida* as two ships he had fitted out and also made it clear that he was fitting out more, but boasted that he always managed matters so that he could defy anyone to prove that he was fitting them out for use by the Confederate government.

On the question of the Rams, Chapman stated that he had been taken over to the Laird shipyard in the early part of April

1863 by a Captain Morton, overlooker for Messrs Boult, English & Brandon of Liverpool, to see the Rams, which Captain Morton assured him were intended for the Confederacy. At the yard, Chapman noted that the Rams were of immense strength, and could not possibly be intended for anything other than war. More telling than this was Chapman's assertion that while he had been with Bulloch he had met Lieutenant John Randolph Hamilton, son of Governor Hamilton of South Carolina, who had stated very clearly that the Rams were being built by Laird & Company for the Confederates.(4)

The issue continued to be the subject of heated public debate throughout the summer of 1863, with correspondence also continuing to fly between Charles Francis Adams and Earl Russell. In perhaps the most significant letter from Adams to Russell, sent on September 16, Adams made it clear that his government had checked out the story put around by Bravary & Company regarding the ships supposedly being built for the Viceroy of Egypt. The French Government had been pressed to apply to the Viceroy to verify Bravary's claims and the answer, as expected, was a complete disavowal of any share in the transaction. More important, Adams made it clear to Russell that the issue of the Laird Rams was putting at risk the peace of their two countries.(5)

## The Government acts

By this date, September 1863, the *El Tousson* was being fitted out in the Alfred Dock, the *El Monassir* still being in Laird's graving dock. However, the message from America that war might be the consequence of letting the Laird Rams leave the Mersey was, at long last, getting through to Palmerston and Russell.

On Thursday 8 October it had been noted in the *Liverpool Mercury* that the Custom House cutter had put an officer aboard the Ram in the Great Float, and that the second vessel, still in the Laird yard, had been boarded the following night. Keen observers had also noted that at about 11pm on the Thursday night HMS *Goshawk*, tender to HMS *Majestic*, had placed herself in a strategic position close to one of the Rams. HMS *Liverpool* had dropped her moorings and cast her anchor immediately opposite the Woodside landing stage – close to the Laird yard. The reporter felt that it was to be regretted that the Government had not adopted a clear and well defined policy regarding these vessels. However, Lairds had not as yet been advised about possible government action concerning the ships.

Two days later, on 10 October, the same paper(6) stated very clearly that the ships should not be allowed to leave the Mersey, as a Tory shipbuilder could not be allowed to put the peace of the nation at risk by his actions. It pointed out that the same yard had also recently built a Confederate war cruiser which, if not in direct contravention of the sadly deficient Foreign Enlistment Act, in all events had endangered friendly relations with a country with which Britain was at peace.(7)

However, the Foreign Enlistment Act was at last found strong enough to justify action against Laird Brothers, who received this note, citing the Act, on 27 October 1863:

"S. Price Edwards, Collector of Customs, Liverpool, to Laird Bros.

"Custom House, Liverpool, 27th October, 1863

"Gentlemen, – I hereby beg to inform you, that your two Cupola Vessels are now detained, under the 223 section of 'The Customs Consolidated Act', the ground of detention being a violation of 'The Foreign Enlistment Act'. And I take leave further to state, that the officers in charge have received directions to remove your workmen at once from on board the ships.

"I am, Gentlemen, your obedient Servant.

(Signed) S. Price Edwards, Collector(8)"

John and William Laird lost no time in responding to this and subsequent actions, sending an indignant telegram to Earl Russell on 29th. In this they stated that Captain Inglefield had just informed them that his orders were to take the two ironclads into the Mersey. Pleading that one of the vessels was a mere hulk, without masts, funnel or steering gear, and the other far from complete, and that taking them out into the river would therefore put their property at risk, they hoped that the orders sent to Captain Inglefield would be reconsidered. Later the same day a telegram came back from the Assistant Secretary at the Treasury, advising the brothers that Captain Inglefield would no doubt take good care of their property, but the orders had been well considered and could not be revoked or altered.(9)

Events now moved rapidly to a conclusion. On 2 November, the local press noted that the public were already aware that Custom House officers and marines had been in possession of both Rams for about a fortnight; but that few were prepared for what happened next, that the workmen were to be "turned adrift" and the Rams moored alongside HMS *Majestic* in the Sloyne. The *El Tousson* was actually towed out of the Great Float on 1 November, the *El Monassir* joining her in the Sloyne on 9th. Captain Inglefield's 'Blue Jackets' were now on board both ships, to ensure that there was no possibility of a repetition of the *Alabama*'s rapid departure.(10)

As soon as the vessels were impounded, Bravary & Company appealed to the Emperor Napoleon to intervene and request the release of the Rams as the property of subjects of France. Napoleon, however, refused to take any action, putting the interests of his nation before those of Messrs Bravary. A suit was then instituted for their forfeiture, but the case was never pushed, and the infamous Rams were then sold to the British Admiralty – a solution to the delicate international situation proposed by Palmerston.(11)

Interestingly, the vessels were valued by the Lords of the Admiralty at £110,000 each, which some observers considered to be £30,000 above their actual value. Despite the fact that the ships were supposedly the property of Bravary & Company, over

£180,000 of this amount promptly reverted to the Confederacy. The loss of these ships to the Confederate States was a severe blow, for there can be no doubt that such formidable men-of-war would have had little difficulty in raising the Federal blockade of the South.

In service with the Royal Navy, the vessels were not used for the purpose for which they had been designed. They proved to be very wet and uncomfortable ships on which to serve. The vessels were not safe as ocean cruisers, rolling a great deal even in a moderate sea. They were also very expensive to operate under steam due to heavy coal consumption, and when under sail performed very badly. At best, it was felt they should only have been used for lake defence in Canada, or harbour defence at home.(12)

# CHAPTER 7

## THE TIDE TURNS AGAINST THE CONFEDERACY

Whilst the loss of the Laird Rams was a severe blow to the naval aspirations of the Confederacy, this was nothing compared to the military setbacks they were now having to endure in America. The day after the decisive victory at Gettysburg, the joy of the North was increased by the news that Vicksburg had surrendered to Grant. Five days later, on 9 July, Port Hudson surrendered and the Mississippi, as Lincoln later put it, "flowed unvexed to the sea". Later in the year, on 24 November, the Battle of Chattanooga was fought in the engagement known as the 'Battle above the Clouds' when the Confederates were driven from the ridge and fell back to Dalton, Georgia with General Sheridan in hot pursuit, capturing thousands of prisoners.(1)

However, all of this did nothing to inhibit the activities of the Confederate raiders *Alabama* and *Florida*, which continued to prowl the high seas in search of Federal victims. Confederate supporters also continued to prowl around Liverpool, actively in search of Abolitionist or pro-Lincoln meet-ings, which they infiltrated and disrupted with boundless enthusiasm.

## The *Florida* at Brest

After taking many valuable prizes in the Atlantic, the *Florida* reached Pernambuco, Brazil on 8 May 1863, and then cruised along the great routes of commerce off that coast, burning more Federal ships. It was near here that Maffitt had made a tender of the brig *Clarence*, and then worked his way back to St George's, Bermuda, where he arrived on 16 July 1863. In all he had now destroyed 14 prizes, and bonded three.(2)

On 25 July the *Florida* sailed from Bermuda, and on 6 August captured the clipper ship *Francis B. Cutting*, homeward bound to New York under the command of Captain J.T. Maloney. The clipper was carrying over 200 passengers, too many for the raider to accommodate, so Maffitt bonded her and allowed her to continue on her way. On 20 August Maffitt captured and destroyed the ship *Anglo Saxon*, and two days later captured another clipper ship, the *Southern Rights*, which, like the *Cutting*, was bound for New York and carrying many passengers; Maffitt bonded her also.

After this eventful crossing the *Florida* arrived at Brest, France, on 23 August, where she was to remain six months in the government's docks, refitting and recruiting. Very soon after the arrival of the *Florida* at Brest, Maffitt's health completely gave way. An attack of yellow fever at Cardenas had left him in a weak state, and subsequent exposure brought on what Bulloch was to describe as 'rheumatism of the heart'. Whilst he was in Bermuda, before crossing over to Europe, Maffitt had informed the Confederate Secretary of the Navy that he would feel bound to obtain a relief when the *Florida* got to Europe, if he did not feel better. On arrival at Brest he felt even worse, so as soon as he had the repair arrangements in hand he resigned his command. Fortunately for the Confederacy, several of their naval officers were then in Paris, one being Commander J.N. Barney, who was designated to relieve Maffitt. As it transpired, Maffitt remained on duty for some time after his arrival in France, dealing with all matters relating to his ship, while Barney was held in reserve.

Immediately upon his arrival at Brest Maffitt reported to the Préfet Maritime, Vice Admiral Conte de Gueyton, explaining to him why he had been compelled to seek shelter in a French port. The Admiral replied that the ship might receive coals and other supplies, and effect necessary repairs, on the same conditions as any 'merchant ship'. This was an interesting position for the Admiral to take, for it was obvious to all that the *Florida* was a fully equipped man-of-war.

However, Conte de Gueyton was not being as generous as appeared from his initial offer, for his interpretation of the term 'necessary repairs' was limited, and did not embrace the concept of a major refit which the ship now required, her engines in particular being in a very poor state. James Dunwoody Bulloch was contacted in Liverpool, and promptly sent a representative of the builders of the ship and engines to Brest to examine the *Florida* and report on her condition. At this point serious amounts of money must have changed hands, for although there was no commercial dock at Brest, permission was eventually given to use a Government dock! Permission was also given to land the small arms to be overhauled by a local gunsmith, although application to land some of the gun-carriages for the same purpose was refused.

The repairs at Brest occupied several months, but whilst this had been going on Maffitt had felt "compelled" to discharge a large number of his men at the port. He gave each of them sufficient money to get to Liverpool only, whilst at the same time informing them that they would not be entitled to be paid their wages in full, unless they "returned" to the Confederate States. This looked like a thinly disguised ploy to avoid paying the men their full wages. They were, however, assured that they would be "directed on the subject" by Captain James Dunwoody Bulloch on arrival at Liverpool. Although Bulloch reports this interesting episode in his narrative, he does nothing to explain how he did actually resolve this management problem.(3)

The next problem facing Maffitt and Bulloch was how to replace these men. Application was made to the French authorities for leave to fill up the vacancies. Unknown to them at the time, this issue was then the subject of much correspondence between Dayton, the United States Minister, and M. Drouyn de l'Huys, the French Minister of Foreign Affairs. The matter was discussed by the

Imperial Cabinet, but the final outcome of these deliberations did not satisfy Confederate requirements, the Government having concluded that they would not prohibit "an accession to the crew, inasmuch as such accession was necessary to her navigation". Put another way, they could engage men only in order to get the ship out of Brest, but this permission did not carry with it the right to enlist men for the Confederate service.

Apart from this, the *Florida* really required English-speaking seamen, who could only be obtained in England – in contravention of the Foreign Enlistment Act. To get round this problem Bulloch engaged men in small groups – 'wherever they could be found' – who were then forwarded to Calais and other French channel ports, and thence by rail to Brest. According to Bulloch the men could not actually be told what they were wanted for until they got on board the *Florida*, although one could be forgiven for doubting his version of events.

Needless to say, the continual movement of groups of nautical-looking men across England and France, with a 'minder' taking charge of each group, soon attracted the attention of several United States consuls who did their utmost to foil these plans. With all of these matters to attend to it is not surpising that the *Florida* was detained a long time at Brest. In the meantime the health of Commander Barney became the matter of much concern, for he was not a strong man. By early January 1864 he was so feeble that he in turn was compelled to retire, to be relieved of his command by Lieutenant C. Manigault Morris.

Morris finally took to sea on 12 February 1864, took new gun-carriages on board off Belle Isle on 19 February, and proceeded to cruise through the West Indies and north towards the American coast. He touched at Martinique on 26 April for coal and supplies and then called at Bermuda in May, merely to communicate and land a sick officer.

## The mission of the *Kearsage*

Whilst the *Florida* had been at Brest, her sister ship the *Alabama* had been cruising in Far Eastern waters. At the same time Captain John Ancrum Winslow remained afloat on the *Kearsage*, on his roving commission to find and destroy the Confederate commerce raiders – in particular the *Alabama* and the *Florida*. His health too was in poor shape: not only did he continue to suffer from chills and fever but more seriously, for want of rest and proper medical attention, he had now completely lost the sight in his right eye.

Dedicated to the cause of the North and the abolition of slavery, Winslow remained on duty, finding his principal comfort at this time in the response his religious services evoked from the crew of the *Kearsage*. It pleased him that the men always seemed to look forward to Sundays with interest, and assembled themselves without being ordered. Perhaps the men did enjoy Winslow's services; they may on the other hand have been showing both respect and sympathy for a mariner who, though clearly not fit to be on active service, chose to remain at his post despite his very considerable suffering.

Winslow left his cruising area off the Azores in the autumn of 1863, making his way to Europe. This enabled him to keep a vigilant watch on the Confederate ironclad building plans then in hand at Nantes, Bordeaux and Birkenhead. He was also aware of the fact that the *Alabama* and *Florida* were by now in need of a complete overhaul, which would probably only be possible in Europe. *En route* from the Azores the *Kearsage* touched at Ferrol, Spain, and whilst there Winslow heard that Maffitt had taken the *Florida* into Brest. He at once reported the situation to the Navy Department, requesting that extra cruisers be sent, as there were three channels leading out of Brest, and it was clear that the *Kearsage* would not be able to watch all of them. But no cruisers came, for the American State Department seems to have felt that the fewer men-of-war America kept in European waters the less likelihood there would be of upsetting the delicate state of international relations with Britain and France.

The autumn and winter of 1863 dragged on. Whilst the *Florida* was being fitted out at Brest, the Federal spies engaged by the United States consul kept Winslow constantly informed on her progress. However, in January 1864 Winslow found it necessary to leave Brest for Cadiz for much needed naval stores and a new suit of sails he was expecting from the United States. Reports from the Federal spies led him to believe that´he would be back on duty long before the *Florida* was ready for sea. Although the *Kearsage* was only away for a month there is no evidence that Lieutenant Morris, the new commander of the *Florida*, was aware of her withdrawal from Brest. Nevertheless, he put to sea in February 1864, one week before Winslow returned.

The completion of engine repairs, and a very strong intimation from the Admiral of the port to leave within 24 hours of this – in accordance with neutrality regulations – were the real reasons for the *Florida* leaving ahead of schedule. Once more a Confederate raider had escaped an engagement with a Federal man-of-war, this time certainly more by good luck that good management. However, even if the *Kearsage* had been off Brest at the time of the *Florida*'s midnight departure, Winslow's chances of intercepting and destroying her would have been slim. He could only have watched one of the three exit channels, and even if by good fortune he had placed his ship on the one chosen by Morris, the darkness might have cheated him of an engagement.(4)

## The *Alabama* in temperate climes

The closing months of 1863 were not particularly pleasant for Maffitt and the crew of the *Florida*, and even less so for Winslow and his crew on the *Kearsage* – cruising in the cold waters of the English Channel. In contrast, Raphael Semmes and his crew seemed to be enjoying themselves enormously, cruising under blue skies in Far Eastern Waters. After leaving the Cape they made the run of 5,000 miles to the Straits of Sunda very quickly. Early in October they found themselves in sight of the two small islands, the largest of which was St Pauls at which they had intended to stop, but bad weather prevented this. They pressed on, passing through the doldrums, before catching the South East Trade Winds which carried them to Sunda. On the last leg of this long passage the crew were kept busy drilling, so that they would be well prepared for the next round of burning and looting which lay ahead of them.

It was whilst on this last leg of their voyage that they spoke and communicated by boat with an English barque, just out of the strait. By this encounter the Confederates received some more up-to-date news about the war in America, which Alabama officer Lieutenant Arther Sinclair mentions in his book without elaboration, no doubt because it would have focused attention on more Confederates losses, and the fact that he and his fellow officers were now, in all probability, acting on behalf of a lost cause. Ostensibly uninhibited by this, they pretended that their interest lay only in the news that the United States cruiser *Wyoming* was holding the passage of the Straits, leaving just occasionally to get coal at Batavia.(5)

Further information offered to Semmes by neutrals indicated that the *Wyoming* had adopted the practice of mooring at night to a buoy off Krakatoa, a volcanic island athwart the passage of the Straits, the currents being too dangerous to move about at night. Semmes took this factor into account, but stuck to his policy of avoiding any direct confrontation with a Federal warship. They cruised about, looking for the immense American fleet of China clippers then famous throughout the world, but found few, for which they took the credit. The truth was that the risk of encounter with a Confederate raider had forced up insurance rates, and also made merchants reluctant to ship in American vessels. The once proud American clipper fleet was, in the main, laid up and rotting in Eastern ports. But a few American

*First Lieutenant and Executive Officer, John McIntosh Kell of The Alabama*

clippers still remained to be taken, which pleased Sinclair, who declared at this point "But still we are not happy. We want to burn something." His wish came true on 6 November when they took their first ship in Eastern waters – the *Amanda* of Boston, bound from Manila to Queenstown with a cargo of sugar. She was condemned and burned, after being looted of attractive stores.

Soon after this incident, Semmes decided to take a chance on getting past the *Wyoming* and out into the South China Seas, where he felt the pickings might be richer. Just at the point where the strait meets the China Sea, they saw through the mist of a rain-squall a truly magnificent vessel, the celebrated American clipper-ship *Winged Racer* under full sail. But the chase was short, the *Alabama* herself being well rigged and having the advantage of steam to add to her speed. Like a cat playing with a mouse, Semmes took his time over sending her to the bottom. He anchored her near North Island, and took the greater part of the night looting her of all the required items before putting her to the torch.(6)

The captain of the doomed vessel requested Semmes to allow him and his crew to make for Batavia in the boats, which Semmes agreed to, on condition that he took with him the prisoners taken from the *Amanda*. They afterwards heard that he arrived safely, no doubt complaining loudly to the local American consul about how much the absence of the *Wyoming* had cost him. The *Wyoming* had actually been away from the Straits at this time in order to obtain coal.

Semmes' next encounter was with the American clipper-ship *Contest*, bound from Yokahama to New York with a varied and very valuable cargo. Vessel and cargo together were worth over $122,000; both were promptly put to the torch. The *Alabama* now steered for the Carimata Strait, another channel taken by the China fleet, in the hope of being able to find and destroy more American clippers. They encountered many ships, but none flying the Stars and Stripes. They did board the British ship *Avalanche*, homeward bound from Singapore; and for a consideration the captain of this vessel agreed to take their prisoners to the nearest point convenient for him, where an American consul was located. This English skipper told them that American commerce was now approaching zero, which was the only consolation they had, for his other news was of the "tightening of the folds of the anaconda" around the Confederacy. Each batch of newspapers they obtained brought further gloom to Semmes and his crew, as the inevitable fate of the Confederacy now began to dawn on them. However, the human capacity for self-delusion is neatly encapsulated in Sinclair's words on the 'wrongs' imposed on the South by the Federal Government: "Do you wonder that the would-be generous impulses of our soul, yearning to stretch out to our brother in his deep affliction, should be smothered in their very birth and fade away at the approach of the solemn funeral march of the wrongs imposed on us?"

Meeting with little further success in these waters the *Alabama* then weighed anchor and set off for the coast of Borneo. She stopped for a few days off this coast and then set sail for the coast of Cochin China, an area where more splendid ships have been wrecked on the reefs and shoals of the lower China Seas than in all the rest of the world. Because of these dangers, Semmes navigated with great care, but the risks of cruising in these dangerous waters did not pay off, as they found no more Federal ships. It was now late November, and Semmes took the decision to head for the island of Condore, then a French settlement of recent acquisition. Here the crew enjoyed themselves for two weeks, hunting and shooting, before continuing their cruise. They hoisted the screw, let the steam go down, and proceeded under a heavy press of canvas towards Singapore in the Straits of Malacca.

This British possession was then noted as the stopping place of the Peninsular & Oriental Company's steamers. The first news that greeted the *Alabama* here was that they had been playing fast and loose with the *Wyoming*. She had followed or anticipated the *Alabama* wherever the latter had been, but somehow managed to miss an encounter with the raider. In his account, Sinclair is here at great pains to point out that all on board the *Alabama* would really have liked to ''try issues with this pursuer'' – although their real ''triumph'' was not to meet, or even destroy her, but to elude and defy her.

The *Alabama* obtained coals and other supplies, and whilst in port the crew went ashore for rest and recreation. Pushing their luck to the extreme, they made their way to the American Bar, at which hotel-cafe the representatives of the great American clipper-fleet were to be found. Twenty-two American clippers were rotting away at their anchors, unable to obtain cargoes due to the reluctance of merchants to ship goods on American vessels; the shipowners themselves were unwilling to risk their vessels with insurance which was hard, if not impossible, to obtain.

The Confederate party of some four or five in number had a drink in the bar, and then went into the billiard parlour to enjoy a game. Unexpectedly they were then approached by a group of American skippers, who offered them hospitality – or appeared to! One of the American skippers then proposed a toast which was clearly an insult to the Confederates. This at once, according to Sinclair, ''called the hot blood into play''. A fight broke out which culminated in a cab race, with the police chasing the Confederates back to the *Alabama*. Sinclair maintained that the Confederates came out best in the fight, though others no doubt saw things differently. Be that as it may, the incident stirred up the whole American colony at Singapore who, in conjunction with the American consul, began to plot the downfall of Semmes and his motley crew. The Confederates sensed that they were being enticed to stay until the *Wyoming* arrived.

Interestingly, the tone of the British colonial press had now changed, for in Singapore it was now highly critical of the activities of the *Alabama*. The press goaded Semmes by charging him with being bold and industrious in burning defenceless merchant ships, but wary and crafty as a fox in skulking from the presence of a man-of-war of equal power. Although Semmes was no coward, he was indeed being obliged by Confederate policy to play the role of one, but despite a probably bruised ego he 'stuck to his guns' – or rather, on Confederate orders, avoided an engagement with the enemy's.

Early on 24 December 1863 the *Alabama* left Singapore, after doing some more recruiting (again, in contravention of the Foreign Enlistment Act). After some four hours' sailing they spotted a distant sail. They soon came up with with the vessel, and hove her to with a blank cartridge. Her build suggested she was an American clipper, but she was flying the English ensign at her peak. Master's Mate Fulham was sent on board of her, and reported that she was the English ship *Martaban* – the name of the Brocklebank Indiaman trading in those waters at this time.(7)

Full of suspicion about this vessel the gig was manned; and for the first and last time on the cruise of the *Alabama* Semmes assumed the part of a boarding officer. From all accounts there was then a very stormy scene on board the *Martaban*. The papers seemed in order, but the skipper and officers were clearly American. Semmes came to the conclusion that the ship was sailing under false colours. The decision was taken to destroy her, and she was promptly prepared for the torch. Under cross examination later, the Captain admitted to Semmes that he was indeed sailing under false colours, and that

the vessel he had just destroyed was the *Texas Star* of Maine.

Having destroyed the 'Down-easter' in disguise on Christmas Eve, the *Alabama* ran in and anchored at nightfall off the little village of Malacca, mainly to offload the prisoners she had just taken. On Christmas morning permission was granted by the English commandant to land these men, and Semmes and his crew spent the remainder of Christmas Day at this anchorage. Their first Christmas of the cruise had been spent at the Arcas Islands in the Gulf of Mexico; now, one year later and on the opposite side of the globe, Semmes and his crew began to reflect sadly on how badly things were going back home for the Confederacy. Sinclair later summed up their feelings at this time in these words:

"What changes have come to the panorama of our lives in the short year! And, meantime, thousands of newly-made graves of our heroes are turfed now by the departed summer, the wounds of the sod healed, leaving those of the widow, parent, and child still open and bleeding. Ah, if this year of toil and success could have brought us evidence of triumph for our cause on home soil! But this was not written in our horoscope."

The days of the Confederacy were indeed distinctly numbered. Whilst the *Alabama* had been occupied in burning American clipper-ships in Eastern waters, Abraham Lincoln had been standing at Gettysburg, looking over the battlefield that had marked the beginning of the end for the Confederate

*Part of the battlefield of Gettysburg*

States. On 20 November 1863, Lincoln stood on this field, and with 15,000 people present made his inspirational Gettysburg Address:

"Fourscore and seven years ago, our fathers brought forth upon this continent a new nation, conceived in liberty and dedicated to the proposition that all men are created equal. Now we are engaged in a great civil war, testing whether that nation – or any nation, so conceived and so dedicated – can long endure. We are met on a great battlefield of that war. We are met to dedicate a portion of it as the final resting place of those who have given their lives that that nation might live. It is altogether fitting and proper that we should do this. But in a larger sense, we cannot dedicate, we cannot consecrate, we cannot hallow, this ground. The brave men, living and dead, who struggled here, have consecrated it, far above our power to add or detract. The world will very little note nor long remember what we say here; but it can never forget what they did here, to the unfinished work that they have thus far so nobly carried on. It is rather for us to be here dedicated to the great task remaining before us; that from these honoured dead we take increased devotion; that we here highly resolve that these dead shall not have died in vain; that the nation shall, under God, have a new birth of freedom, and that government of the people, by the people, for the people, shall not perish from the earth."

Even if Raphael Semmes and his crew had read these words by Christmas 1863, they would not have shared Lincoln's dedication to freedom and democracy. The *Alabama*

moved quickly along now under steam; and just after midday, 26 December, they saw two ships at anchor in the Straits, waiting for a favourable wind. They proved to be the American clippers *Sonora* of Newburyport and the *Highlander* of Boston, bound in ballast from Singapore to Akyad, where they were to load rice for England. They were captured and the torch applied as usual. However, before the ships were burned the two commanders asked Semmes if they could have the ships' boats so that all the officers and crews of the ships could reach Singapore to report the matter to the American consul. As the *Alabama* was not remaining in these waters Semmes was only too pleased to let them all go, as this relieved him of the problem of disposing of yet another batch of prisoners.

## The *Alabama*'s last victims

The *Alabama* had entered the Straits of Sunda on the first day of November, 1863, and re-entered the Indian Ocean on 25 December. The result of her hunt was six United States ships caught and destroyed, all of them first class and very valuable.

The *Alabama* now started to coast along the western side of the island of Sumatra, before letting go for the passage over to India. She met many vessels on the way, but all were sailing under neutral flags. She then doubled the island of Ceylon without so much as the smell of a capture, and continued the cruise by moving along the coast of Malabar. Here the crew spotted an American sail, the unfortunate vessel being the *Emma Jane* of

Bath, Maine. After robbing the ship of all valuable items the crew and passengers were removed, and the torch was applied once more – the first time that the *Alabama* had 'lit up' the Indian Ocean. The prisoners were landed at the small Portuguese settlement of Anjenga.

The raider passed through the doldrums of the equator in late January, and then headed up for the Mozambique Channel, all aboard being aware that they were about to pay a return visit to Cape Town. At this point their information about the war at home was becoming decidedly dated, although any desire to be kept informed must have been mingled with dread, for it was becoming clear to the crew of the *Alabama* that they were fighting for a lost cause. Lieutenant Arthur Sinclair neatly summing up their feelings:

"It is becoming only too plain to us that the resources of our foe are practically boundless, and that we are to be left unaided to cope with them. At last advices, Lee was still breasting the avalanche with his 'Stonewall' brigade. But how long could such a contest last with seaports sealed, homes devastated, and the enemy, with an immensely greater population, abundant means, and the whole earth to draw from, pressing upon us from every side? But it was not ours to utter, even to each other, the doubts we felt. We kept them in our hearts, and talked cheerfully."(8)

General 'Stonewall' Jackson was, in the opinion of many, the best General Lee had. His last great battle had been at Chancellor-ville, Virginia on 6 May 1863, but Jackson had died of wounds received in this battle four days later – an indication of how out of touch Semmes and his crew now were. If they were demoralised by the way the struggle was going on the basis of pre-May information, they might have found it even harder to cope with contemporary events, and in particular the decisive Confederate defeat at Gettysburg. However, their opportunity to face up to reality lay in the not too far distant future.

After entering the Mozambique Channel the raider stood for the island of Comoro near the African coast. Here, at the main harbour Johanna, they ran in and anchored off the town, right below the great cliffs. They took on supplies, and then stood to the southward, bound now for Cape Town. In the first week of March they sounded on the Agulhas Bank, and then cruised off the pitch of the Cape for two weeks, searching, without success, for Federal ships. They then entered the roadstead of Cape Town, where they were to remain for just three days, taking in coals and supplies.

Here at last they received the late newspapers from the seat of the war, from which they noted that the Confederate States appeared to be in the last throes of dissolution. The feelings on board the vessel, at least as expressed later by Sinclair, were that the hostilities should stop. However, the bloody struggle was to continue until 9 April 1865 when Lee eventually surrendered at Appomattox, effectively ending the American Civil War.

At the close of March 1864, the *Alabama* left Cape Town bound for the North Atlantic, standing for the island of St Helena, which was in the regular track of vessels bound to England or the United States. Not a single prize was caught along this busy highway of commerce – none of the many other vessels was sailing under the American flag. On 22 April they found themselves in the track of vessels from the Pacific, and soon spotted an American sail, the ship *Rockingham*. A long chase followed which lasted all night, but when the *Alabama* caught up with her a shot was put across her bows, and she surrendered. She was used as target practice before being consigned to the torch.

On 27 May the *Alabama* was near the equator once more when the crew spotted the magnificent American clipper-ship *Tycoon*, bound from New York to San Francisco with a large and valuable assorted cargo; ship and cargo together were worth over $88,000. Following normal practice the ship was robbed of all valuable items, the passengers and crew transferred, and the ship consigned to the torch. But this was to be the last victim of the Laird-built Confederate raider *Alabama*. Since her career had begun she had captured in all 68 United States vessels, bonding some, but destroying the vast majority of these unarmed merchantmen.

During the month of May they only encountered neutral ships, from whom they received the latest news confirming the futility of their cause. Undeterred, the *Alabama* raced along to face her final destiny. On 10 June, she entered the English Channel and the next day entered the harbour at Cherbourg. The cruise of the *Alabama* had ended. Waiting for her was Captain Winslow of the *Kearsage*. Now half-blind and ill, he remained on duty, hoping that destiny would allow him to destroy the *Alabama*, the vessel which epitomised all that he most detested.

## The Reverend Henry Beecher in Liverpool

Whilst the *Alabama* had been cruising in the Far East much had been happening in Europe. Confederate wrecking activity reached something of a climax in Liverpool during October, 1863: the focus of attention and hatred was the famous American preacher and abolitionist, the Reverend Henry Ward Beecher, who had come to Liverpool to address a gathering of supporters at the Philharmonic Hall.

Beecher was the son of the Reverend Lyman Beecher, a minister at Lichfield, Connecticut. Trained for the ministry under his father, Henry became a Presbyterian minister, later becoming an outspoken abolitionist and perhaps in his day the most popular preacher in the United States. He also won a reputation as a lecturer, and both preached and lectured in England. His sister was Harriet Elizabeth Beecher Stowe, the author of the most famous piece of anti-slavery propaganda ever written, *Uncle Tom's Cabin*.(9) This book, first serialised in 1851 in the *National Era*, a Washington DC paper, appeared in book form in 1852, and within a year reached sales of 300,000 copies. It consolidated anti-slavery opinion in the North, deeply angered the South, and has to be considered as one of the factors bringing on the American Civil War.(10) Whilst the anticipated arrival of Beecher, a man with such impeccable abolitionist credentials, was eagerly awaited by his thousands of supporters and admirers in Liverpool who planned a warm reception for him, the Confederates elements laid plans to wreck this reception.

For several days before the meeting it was understood that efforts would be made to create a disturbance there. The Confederates clearly had friends in high places, for it was noted that those responsible for maintaining law and order in the town had departed from their usual policy of preserving order at public meetings. Placards had been issued well in advance of the meeting calling upon the people of Liverpool to give Mr Beecher an uncivil reception, proving conclusively that influences were being exercised to create a 'scene' at the proposed meeting; yet no special measures were taken to keep order.

The meeting took place at the Philharmonic Hall on Friday 16 October. As soon as the doors were opened a huge crowd moved in, and within minutes all the seats were taken. Observant reporters from the local press noticed that amongst those present were several gentlemen whose features were familiar at the Liverpool Southern Club Room. However, these gentlemen remained quiet during the proceedings, leaving the orchestrated disruption that was to follow to their dupes. The entrance of a negro, who was conducted to a conspicuous seat on the platform, was the signal for a violent outburst of party feelings, intermingled with cries of 'Sambo', hooting, yells, and cheers. This pattern of behaviour continued throughout the meeting. The arrival of the Reverend Beecher prompted deafening cheers, but the vocal minority of Confederate dupes hissed and booed to the best of their ability. Despite the interruptions, Beecher eventually rose and spoke to the huge meeting. He explained to the audience that such was the hatred of abolitionists in the South that for the past 25 years there had not been a single day of his life when it would have been safe for him to pass south of the Mason-Dixon Line in his own country, and all for one reason: his solemn, earnest, persistent testimony against what he considered to be the most atrocious thing under the sun – the system of American slavery in a great free republic.

He pointed out that in the South, no matter what injury a coloured man might receive, he was not allowed to appear in court nor to testify against a white man. It was also a penitentiary offence to teach a black man to read and to write; but in the North many hundreds of thousands of dollars were spent to teach black people, who had their own schools, acadamies, churches, and lawyers.

On the sensitive issue of neutrality, he stated that he did not agree with the doctrine of neutrality in the past as a mere question of law, but it had passed, and he was not disposed to raise that question. However, the Government action of stopping the war steamers in the Mersey had gone far towards quieting every fear and apprehension from the hearts of the Americans. At this a lone voice rang out ''Three cheers for Messrs Laird & Company'' – to which the response seems to have been limited.

The meeting was eventually brought to a close by the Reverend Birrell who gave a vote of thanks to Beecher, and somewhat optimistically stated that he expected his vote of thanks would be enthusiastically joined in by all the representatives of American slaveowners at the meeting. After a motion had been put by John Patterson the assembly then separated, but Beecher was detained for some considerable time on the platform by his friends, who crowded round him, wishing him well.(11)

Before he left Liverpool a 'Farewell Breakfast' was arranged for Beecher, organised by the Liverpool Emancipation Society. It was held in St James's Hall, Lime Street, on the morning of Friday 30 October. Here, many more comments were made concerning the activity of local pro-Confederacy elements. In his long opening address, Mr C. Wilson, President of the Emancipation Society, had some particularly scathing comments to make about the builder of the Confederate Raider *Alabama*, John Laird:

''They have had Mr Laird for their shipbuilder, they might have sought England through and not found such another; not only has he built them ships which cannot be surpassed, but he has sacrificed for them his parliamentary reputation, making unverified statements which have been repudiated with scorn. If

*John Laird (Liverpool Central Library)*

*69, Hamilton Sq., Birkenhead; the residence of John Laird in the 1860s. (Chris Sarson)*

Mr Laird had any hankering after a Northern contract, he certainly did not seek the front door. The next time he makes a pretended statement of facts in parliament he will be reminded of these anonymous letters, and will not find it so easy to ride off on a piece of empty clap-trap about Mr John Bright, MP, setting class against class.

"These shores do not contain a nobler or a purer patriot than John Bright. Mr Laird may say that he would rather be known as the builder of the *Alabama* than as he; but I venture to predict that the name of John Bright will be honoured, and cherished, and loved by all the English nation when the name of the builder of the *Alabama*, if remembered at all, will be as that of a man who, to fill his own pockets with gold, not only violated the proclamations of his sovereign but did his utmost to bring two kindred nations into collision, to cover sea and land with fire and blood, and to involve the whole British race in all the horrors and calamities of war."(12)

## The Confederate 'White Elephant'

A few weeks after this meeting at which so much was said about John Laird, builder of the Confederate States most successful raider, the least successful of the South's raiders was brought into service. She was the *Rappahannock*, which had a very brief career. She was originally the dispatch boat *Victor* of the British navy, a screw steamer of 500 tons burthen, and had proved so defective that the Government sold her at auction on 10 November 1863. She was bought secretly by a representative of the Confederacy under the pretence that she was to be engaged in the China trade. After the sale the vessel remained at Sheerness, refitting under the direction of persons connected with the Royal Dockyard. Suspicions were soon aroused as to her true ownership and character, it being concluded that she was destined for the Confederate service. The British Foreign Office acted promptly, issuing an order that she was to be detained.(13)

However, on 24 November, a young Scotsman named Ramsey succeeded in running her out of Sheerness, her departure being even more rapid than the departure of the *Alabama* from the Mersey. So hastily was she put to sea that many astonished workmen were still in her when she raced away. Even more amazing was the fact that she only had part of her crew on board, and that these had been enlisted by the Inspector of Machinery at the dockyard – no doubt for a substantial consideration.(14)

Passing down the Thames the brasses of the *Rappahannock* blew out, thus confirming the wisdom of the British Government in disposing of the vessel. She then drifted over the Channel in the general direction of France. In mid-Channel she was put in commission as a Confederate man-of-war, with the usual pomp and ceremony. She continued to drift aimlessly until she was near Calais, at which point her anchor was let go, and she then claimed admission to the port as a ship-of-war in distress and needing repairs. The impudence of this demand was too much

even for the most sympathetic of neutrals. However, she was allowed to enter the port. Lieutenant Fauntleroy, CSN was then ordered to take command of her by Commander Barron, the Naval Agent of the Confederacy at Paris.

*John Bright, MP*

After the *Rappahannock* had made some attempts to enlist more men and to continue her preparations for sea, her operations were summarily ended by a French gunboat, which was stationed across her bows. These significant points were not mentioned in Scharf's account of events concerning the vessel. He merely stated that a survey had found her unsuited for a cruiser – although he acknowledges that she remained manned, and ready for duty! No explanation was offered to explain this contradiction.

Her only real use to the Confederacy was to keep one or two Federal vessels off Calais, watching her to see that she did not go to sea. However, one of these vessels was the *Kearsage*, Winslow finding this responsibility an extra burden.(15) Boxed in, the ill-fated *Rappahannock* remained at Calais until the news of the surrender of General Lee was received, when Lieutenant Fauntleroy was ordered to pay off the officers and crew and turn the vessel over to James Dunwoody Bulloch. Fauntleroy appropriately called her ''The Confederate White Elephant''.

## Prosecutions in Liverpool

Throughout the remainder of 1863 and into 1864 Liverpool continued to be the base for Confederate activity, virtually all of it orchestrated by Messrs Fraser, Trenholm & Company and Captain James Dunwoody Bulloch. However, by the winter of 1863-64 public opinion was well set against them, with the local press, and in particular the *Liverpool Mercury*, doing much to expose them with critical coverage of Confederate activity in Liverpool in January 1864, recruiting for the Confederate navy.

Rumours had been rife in the town for some time concerning Confederate recruiting in the port, actions which should have brought those responsible within the scope of the Foreign Enlistment Act. Making an oblique reference to the activity of the Laird family, the *Mercury*'s reporter noted that not only had the friends of the Southern states succeeded in negotiating for the sale and building of ships for the ''Emperor of China'' and other equally distinguished potentates with impunity, under the very nose of the authorities; but they had also, in some instances, been endeavouring to recruit for the Confederacy. There had, the paper maintained, been abundant evidence to ''criminate'' more than one person in acts which to say the least were inimical to the spirit of the Foreign Enlistment Act; but after the seizure of the 'Rams' it had not been considered judicious to proceed further in the matter. ''Reasons'' had been found as to why it would have been injudicious to proceed against the rich and powerful.

Fraser, Trenholm & Company, James Dunwoody Bulloch, John Laird and his family were not prosecuted under the terms of the Foreign Enlistment Act, but eventually action was taken in Liverpool against the 'small-fry' further down the line. The case brought to court in Liverpool in January 1864 was connected with the Confederate cruiser *Georgia*, and the full force of the law was brought to bear against Messrs Jones & Company, shipstore dealers, 38 Chapel

Street. Thomas Wilding, one of their clerks, was prominent among the accused. Throughout the proceedings no mention was made of Bulloch, or Fraser Trenholm & Company, although it is not on record that Jones & Company of Chapel Street had assumed the role of bankers to the Confederacy, or that Wilding had assumed responsibility for those Confederate duties entrusted to Captain James Dunwoody Bulloch.

Nevertheless, the rusty wheels of British justice were, albeit slowly, turning. Messrs Bateson and Robinson appeared on behalf of the Treasury for the prosecution. The accusations against the defendants were that during the previous year a vessel was built at Dumbarton called the *Japan* (*Georgia*), the sole registered owner at that time being Mr Thomas Bold of Liverpool. Bold then sold the ship to a foreigner. She was manned partly from Liverpool and partly from Greenock. The men concerned were induced to sign articles for a voyage to Singapore and back for two years. They were in the first instance directed to the office of Jones & Company, where they received their advance notes. After they had joined the *Japan* she sailed off, nominally on a trial trip, and after a few days met a small steamer "accidentally", which went with them to Brest. There they took from the steamer guns and ammunition, and Lieutenant Manley came on board, put on the uniform of a Confederate officer, and began recruiting, promising the men good wages and prize money.

The prosecutors alleged that Jones, a member of the defendant's firm, was with Manley when all this happened, and according to the witnesses also took part in the recruiting efforts. Jones presented those who signed up with a £10 bounty, promised to take that money to the men's wives, and gave his undertaking that half of their wages would be paid by him to their wives. However, about 20 of the men refused to sign up, returning with Jones in the supply steamer. The *Georgia* then sailed off, hoisted the Confederate colours, and cruised around the Atlantic destroying American ships. Eventually she returned to Cherbourg, where the men obtained leave to go to Liverpool. After they arrived home, dissatisfaction arose with regard to the payment of their wages. Word soon spread around the port about the issue, and reached the Liverpool-based private detective Maguire, who was employed on a standing arrangement by Dudley, the United States consul. Obligingly, Maguire took these men under his wing, then regularly paid their wages of £1 19s 4d each week for, as they expressed it, "making their statement".

For the defence, it was stated that until the vessel was at Brest no offence had actually been committed, for it was there that the enlistment took place. Mr Raffles, the stipendiary magistrate, said that without expressing an opinion on the merits of the case, he considered it his duty on the evidence before him to bind over the defendant in two sureties to answer any indictment that might be preferred against him at the next assizes. The bail set was very substantial, and eventually justice was done – within the limitations of the Act.(16)

# CHAPTER 8

## THE SINKING OF THE *ALABAMA*

### An encounter looms

When the *Alabama* sailed up the English channel on 10 June 1864, the *Kearsage* was anchored in the Scheldt off Flushing; John Winslow's main concern at the time was to intercept and destroy the Confederate raider *Rappahannock* when she eventually left port. Although she was actually worthless, the Federal Government was not aware of this, and wrongly considered her to pose a considerable threat to United States shipping in the area. With his attention thus concentrated on the *Rappahannock*, Winslow was surprised when, on 12 June, he received a telegram from the local American consul, informimg him that the *Alabama* had just put into Cherbourg. At last he was to have the opportunity to destroy the most notorious of all the Confederate raiders.(1)

Onshore the net was also closing in. Immediately after the arrival of the *Alabama* at Cherbourg an officer was sent ashore with a communication to the Port Admiral, asking permission to land the prisoners of the *Rockingham* and *Tycoon*, the last two cap-

tures, which was promptly granted. Permission was also sought for docking privileges at the only available yard which belonged to the government. No immediate response could be given to this request as only the Emperor could give such permission, and he was on holiday at Biarritz.(2)

In the meantime the United States Minister William L. Dayton contacted Seward, advising him that he had telegraphed Captain Winslow, then at Flushing, who had replied that he would be off Cherbourg about Wednesday. In the same note he also wrote that he had lodged a protest with M. Drouyn de Lhuys, Minister of Foreign Affairs, objecting to any facilities being extended to the *Alabama*. He concluded by stating that the arrival of *Alabama* would spread universal dismay among American shippers and all engaged in American trade.(3)

On 14 June, three days after the *Alabama* had entered the harbour at Cherbourg, the USS *Kearsage* swept dramatically into the harbour, came to a rapid halt, and without even anchoring sent a boat on shore; moments later she steamed out to sea again, stopping just outside the breakwater. The sole object of her visit seemed to be to receive on board, or at least make contact with, the prisoners landed by the *Alabama*. There was no danger to Semmes of being attacked in the French port, for international law would not have allowed such action.(4)

On 17 June Dayton wrote to Seward again, informing him that on the previous day he and Drouyn de Lhuys had agreed that the *Alabama* would not be allowed to remain at

Cherbourg. They had also noted the arrival of the *Kearsage* off the port and the danger of an imminent fight between the two vessels. The Minister's main concern was that any fight should be conducted well outside French territorial waters.

Interestingly, this note also stated that the *Alabama* had expressed its readiness to fight. Semmes had actually taken his ship to France for repair; a battle with a United States man-of-war was against his standing orders.(5) It was only now – when the French were making it clear to Semmes that he was not welcome, and that the *Alabama* would not be allowed to remain in port – that Semmes decided to cast himself in the role of a gallant knight, wishing to go forth and do battle with another knight of equal standing. According to one of his Lieutenants, Arthur Sinclair, Semmes now lost no time after the appearance of the *Kearsage* in obtaining from Commodore Samuel Barron, the officer in charge of naval matters abroad, permission to offer the *Kearsage* battle!

In truth, having been ordered by the Minister of Foreign Affairs to leave Cherbourg, whether Semmes liked it or not he would have to confront the *Kearsage* – and more Federal ships if he waited. His only other option – to remain in port and desert the ship – would have involved Semmes and the Confederate cause in too much loss of face. After losing at Gettysburg, the South needed a morale booster, not another humiliation, and what would be better than for the 'legendary' *Alabama* to sink the Federal ship *Kearsage*? Word now spread like wildfire

around Europe about the 'gallant challenge' made by Semmes which, as Semmes well knew, naval regulations prevented Winslow from acknowledging. Nevertheless, thousands of excited people now began to make their way to Cherbourg, anxious to witness the great battle. Amongst those making this journey was the noted French Impressionist, Edouard Manet, intent on painting the event.

Captain Winslow now received an important communication from William Dayton, delivered by Dayton's son, and informing him that Drouyn de Lhuys had given the *Alabama* notice to leave Cherbourg, and that a fight was expected between the Federal and Confederate vessels. The minister was insistent that no battle should take place in French waters, but if the *Alabama* could be taken without violating any rules of international law, and without upsetting the French, he knew what the United States Government expected of him. The letter concluded by advising Captain Winslow that the United States ship *Niagara* would soon be proceeding to European waters, to be followed by the man-of-war *Dictator*. An attached copy letter from the Cabinet of the Minister in Paris dated 15 June, also advised Winslow that the prisoners of the *Alabama* set free on French soil would not be delivered up to the *Kearsage*, as this would be considered an augmentation of military force, which they were not prepared to allow.(6)

The French did, however, allow the two master's mates of the *Alabama* to rejoin the Confederate ship. These were the European aristocrats, Baron Maximilian Von Meulnier

*Captain Winslow and The Kearsage*

Paris. The Cherbourg hotels and lodging houses were soon full to capacity, but the crowds kept arriving. The duel to the death between the representatives of the United States and the Confederacy was to be watched by vast numbers of people, crowding the headlands to witness the historic event.

The Laird-built yacht *Deerhound*, built for the Duke of Leeds but now owned by John Lancaster of Hindley Hall, Wigan and commanded by Captain E. P. Jones, also arrived in Cherbourg before the day of the battle. Lancaster and his family joined the vessel on 18th, when a family consultation was held as to whether they should go out and witness the fight. The vote was even when the youngest child Catherine, aged nine, cast the final decisive vote in favour of watching the duel. Thus it was that a child became the instrument of saving many Confederate lives, and gave her family a place in history.

As the hour of battle approached the French officials were studiously polite, but distant and reserved, towards Semmes and his crew, doubtless reflecting government instructions. However, according to Sinclair the Port Admiral informed Semmes a day or so before the fight that an officer detailed to visit the *Kearsage* in the offing had reported that heavy protective chain armour was draped over the side of the ship; he strongly advised Semmes not to engage her, and that only good luck could throw the scales in his favour. But for Semmes this was advice which he could no longer afford to take: he had been accused of being a pirate and a

and Julius Schroeder, who escaped the ruling because they had started home on leave after the *Alabama* had arrived at Cherbourg, and had got as far as Paris when, learning that the fight was to take place, they returned at once and were allowed to rejoin their ship. In this case they were considered not to be augmenting the crew of the ship, but to be merely men on leave reporting back to their vessel.

The men-of-war entered the arena on the morning of Sunday 19 July, by which date news of the battle had spread around not only Europe, but indeed the whole world – wired to every major city with telegraphic facilities. Excursion trains carrying thousands continued to head for Cherbourg from all points of the Continent, particularly from cowardly destroyer of unarmed merchant ships, and now the whole world was watching to see how he would, at long last, stand up to an equal opponent.

Statistically the two ships appear to have been well matched. Their manpower was about equal, although the odds here were slightly against Winslow because all but one of his officers were inexperienced volunteers from the merchant service.(7) The Confederates could bring six guns to bear on a broadside, as against five by the Federal, and the British-built rifles of the *Alabama* outranged those of the *Kearsage*.

In protection, the odds were in favour of the *Kearsage*, for with experience and foresight Winslow had indeed employed a device used to protect Federal gunboats on the Mississippi – that of draping spare chain abeam of the boilers and engine rooms, and boxing them over with light planking. Semmes counted on full coal bunkers to afford similar protection, although there was nothing to prevent him from using his own chains in a similar way – particularly as he was forewarned about this strategy employed by Winslow. After the battle Semmes claimed that he did not know about the chains, hidden as they were under planking, and that this had induced him to fight what was in reality an armoured ship. Though himself an experienced attacker of unarmoured merchant ships, Semmes made it clear that he considered Winslow's actions in this respect most unfair – even though, as already noted, Sinclair claimed that he did know about the chain armour of the *Kearsage*.

## The *Alabama* leaves harbour

It was at about 10.30 on the morning of 19 June that the *Alabama* got under way, sailing past the powerful French fleet that occupied the harbour. This included the line-of-battle-ship *Napoleon*, and the iron-clad *Couronne*. Rather to the surprise of Semmes and his crew, as the *Alabama* sailed past the *Napoleon* they found the crew manning the rigging, and giving the raider three cheers: Sinclair admitted that this must have been "an enthusiasm of local birth, a sort of private turn-out of their own".

They continued through the dense shipping of the harbour, past vessels full of spectators, the shores being a moving mass of humanity. Significantly, Sinclair does not mention that they were cheering the *Alabama* on her way. The day was perfect, with scarcely a breath of air stirring and light clouds in an otherwise clear blue sky, as they made for the open sea. Before they passed out of the harbour, the *Couronne* had weighed anchor and stood out from the harbour, her mission being to guard the three-mile limit; she remained there during the whole engagement, making no attempt later to be involved in rescue work.(8)

The yacht *Deerhound* had steamed out of Cherbourg even earlier in the morning, with the intention of taking up a good vantage point. The crew of the Confederate ship assumed that Lancaster and his family were merely intent on continuing their pleasure cruise.

When the *Alabama* was sighted by the

*Kearsage*, the Federal ship was about three miles offshore; characteristically, the deeply religious Winslow was conducting a divine service before his crew. However, as soon as the look-out confirmed that the *Alabama* was heading towards them he closed the service and beat to quarters with scant ceremony.

Whilst the guns of the *Kearsage* were being cast loose and provided with ammunition, Winslow lay a north-easterly course away from the land, with the *Alabama* on his port quarter. When he had reached a distance of some seven miles off shore, he trained his pivot guns to starboard,and came about to a course that lay almost directly towards the *Alabama*.(9)

## The battle

But it was the *Alabama* which opened the engagement: taking advantage of her longer range guns she let go with her entire starboard battery, to which the *Kearsage* promptly responded. The battle now began in earnest; after about 15 minutes' fighting the *Alabama* managed to lodge a 100-pound percussion shell in the *Kearsage*'s quarter, near her screw, but it failed to explode. As the ships circled, Semmes became aware of the superior speed of the *Kearsage*. He decided then that his best hopes lay in trying to board the *Kearsage*, and attempted to bring about yard-arm quarters, fouling and boarding, relying on his more experienced crew to overpower Winslow's men. This tactic soon became apparent to Winslow, who frustrated it. The failed boarding attempts had brought the heavy guns of the

*Kearsage* dangerously close to the unprotected hull of the *Alabama* and Winslow's crew took advantage of the situation, pouring shot after shot into the enemy. In all the *Kearsage* fired 173 rounds during the battle; how many took effect it is impossible to say, but those that did hull ˉthe *Alabama* did terrible damage.

Soon, the bulwarks of the *Alabama* were shot away in sections, and the spar deck was rapidly torn up by shells bursting on the between decks. The *Alabama* now began to make water fast, and became dull in response to her helm. Two 11-inch shells then hit the *Alabama* between wind and water and quickly brought about the flooding of the engine rooms. The vessel that had sunk so many unarmed ships was at last being sunk herself. Semmes used what power she had left to make a run for it, throwing his ship's head towards the French coast with the intention of running for neutral waters. Winslow altered course and continued to fire with his starboard battery, cutting off the *Alabama*'s line of retreat. A few odd shots came from the *Alabama*, but Semmes was now advised by his engineers that in his new position his fires were being flooded, and that only two guns could be brought to bear.

The Confederate commerce raider was finished, and Semmes knew it. He promptly struck his colours. The men on the *Kearsage* at once ceased firing, but they had no sooner done so than several more shots were fired from the *Alabama*'s port battery. Whether this was duplicity or error, the response was immediate, the *Kearsage* reopening fire with a vengeance. At the same time Winslow put his ship in a raking position athwart the bow of the doomed ship. Within seconds Semmes ran up the white flag.(10)

By 12.20 the *Alabama* was sinking stern foremost, and the water was filled with men struggling to get clear before the suction of the sinking vessel drew them under. Only the wounded had been provided for in the *Alabama*'s few remaining boats when the doomed ship threw her bow high in the air, then slipped below the waves. According to Semmes, the *Kearsage* then "stood sullenly at a distance, making no motion, that we could see to send us a boat".(11) This seems to have been an attempt by Semmes to blacken the character of John Ancrum Winslow, as in fact the boats of both men-of-war had been so badly damaged that rescue work could only progress slowly.

## The role of the *Deerhound*

It was at this point that Lancaster came up close to the *Kearsage*, and was hailed by Winslow and requested to participate in the rescue work. At the same time Winslow apparently made it absolutely clear to Lancaster that he regarded any men whom he did rescue as prisoners of the United States, who should later be handed over to him. At the time of the rescue there is no indication that Lancaster objected to these terms.(12)

The rescue work then commenced, and 42 were rescued by the *Deerhound* including Semmes, Kell, and 11 other officers. Nine were rescued by the French pilot boat, three of whom were officers. Significantly, 70 men were then put aboard the *Kearsage*, but of these only six were officers. It was then that a subordinate brought Winslow's attention to the fact that the *Deerhound* was moving away, instead of bringing the prisoners back to the *Kearsage*, to Winslow's amazement: "I could not believe that her owner would do such a thing."(13)

Later, in a long letter to the press, Lancaster attempted to justify his actions by arguing that he had a legal right to take away Captain Semmes "and his friends" and that the request by Captain Winslow to rescue men had not been coupled with any stipulation to the effect that he should deliver up the rescued to Captain Winslow as prisoners. He had also been led to understand that an English ship was English territory, and that he had a right to deliver up rescued men to a port of his choosing, and not hand them over as prisoners. Although a fair legal argument, this was not an honourable position to take if Winslow had coupled his request to Lancaster to rescue the men of the *Alabama* with an acknowledged understanding from Lancaster that the men would then be handed over to the *Kearsage* as prisoners. Here we are left to decide who is telling the truth – Winslow or Lancaster. It would seem to be out of character for the deeply religious Winslow to have lied about this crucial point, with his officers and crew witnesses to the facts. On the other hand, Lancaster's bias against Winslow and the United States Government as expressed in his own letter is revealing, and may indicate a lack of truthfulness and objectivity:

"What Captain Winslow's notion of

humanity may be is a point beyond my knowledge; but I have good reason for believing that not many members of the Royal Yacht Squadron would, from 'motives of humanity', have taken Captain Semmes from the water in order to give him up to the tender mercies of Captain Winslow and his compatriots.''

Lancaster's implication that Captain Winslow would not have treated his prisoners with respect and humanity had they been handed over was of course a gross slander, as Winslow treated all his prisoners with the greatest of respect and consideration. However, had Semmes and his crew been handed over to Winslow there is no doubt that they would have been put on trial for their actions and, under the influence of Secretary Welles, received harsh sentences.

Needless to say, Charles Francis Adams promptly took up the issue of the *Deerhound* with Earl Russell, writing to him from the Legation of the United States on 25 June. In this note he objected to the interference of a British vessel with a view to effecting the escape of a number of persons belonging to the *Alabama*, who had already surrendered themselves as prisoners of war. Adams also drew his lordship's attention to the remarkable proportion of officers and American insurgents on the *Deerhound*'s list of rescued men, as compared with the total number of those rescued. ''That this selection was made by British subjects with a view to connive' at the escape of these particular individuals from captivity, I can scarcely entertain a doubt.''(15)

Meanwhile, Semmes and his crew were being given V.I.P. treatment in Southampton. On arrival there they were welcomed by Mason, the Confederate Envoy, James Dunwoody Bulloch, and the Reverend Tremlet, all of whom breakfasted with the officers of the *Alabama* at Kelway's Hotel on the morning of Tuesday 21 June. The Southampton correspondent of the *Daily News* was present, who informed his readers that as soon as Semmes had landed on the previous day he had inquired after Mr Alderman Perkins of Southampton, whom Semmes claimed as a personal friend. As it happened Perkins was in London, but when advised about the arrival of Semmes he telegraphed to Southampton, wanting to know if Semmes would accept an invitation to a public dinner at Southampton. Semmes declined,(16) but the 'red carpet' treatment continued to be offered to Semmes by British supporters of the Confederacy.

Semmes proved to be a very poor loser. Years later, complaining bitterly in his memoirs about how unfair the *Kearsage/Alabama* battle had been, with his enemy going out ''chivalrously armoured, to encounter a ship whose sides were entirely without protection... I should have beaten him in the first thirty minutes of the engagement, but for the defect of my ammunition, which had been two years on board.'' Coming from a man who had ''chivalrously'' spent the previous two years attacking unarmed merchant ships whose wooden sides had also been entirely without protection, this was rich indeed.(17) Not content with this vitriolic broadside, Semmes continued his narrative:

"Great rejoicing was had in Yankeedom, when it was known that the *Alabama* had been beaten. Shouts of triumph rent the air, and bonfires lighted every hill. But along with the rejoicing there went up a howl of disappointed rage, that I had escaped being made a prisoner."(18)

## Aftermath

During the next two months the *Kearsage* remained in European waters, where Winslow was acclaimed as the hero of the hour. He took the opportunity to go to Paris – not to be hailed as a hero, but to visit an oculist, who had to inform him that the sight of his right eye had completely gone. Whilst there though he found that, to his surprise, he was a celebrated hero. He was invited to give speeches, attend parties and other such "nonsense" – until he wished that he was back on his ship. In a letter to his wife he stated that all this fuss would have been very gratifying to him when he was young, but now all he wanted was peace and rest.

He was not, however, to get the peace and rest he deserved for some time. Later in the summer the United States men-of-war *Niagara* and *Sacramento* arrived in European waters, the *Kearsage* was relieved, and Winslow set a course for America. But the Confederate raider *Florida* was still afloat, and doing considerable damage to United States shipping. Winslow was instructed to cruise as far south as the coast of South America in seach of the marauder. An involvement with this ship, but not a battle, lay ahead of Winslow before he was to arrive back in the United States to the hero's welcome he had earned.

After a rest in Switzerland, Semmes returned to the Confederacy by way of the 'back door' route through Mexico. He arrived at Richmond in January, 1865, and was assigned as a Rear Admiral to the command of the James River Squadron, which consisted of three ironclad rams and seven wooden steamers. As his anchorage was flanked by powerful shore batteries, Richmond was safe from the Federal fleet; but when the capital was evacuated by the army Semmes was obliged to burn his own ships and turn his men into a naval brigade, which was surrendered at Greensboro as part of Johnson's army.

Kell, the Executive Officer of the *Alabama*, made his way back to the Confederacy by the 'front door' taking a ship that went through the blockade. He was then ordered to the ironclad *Richmond* at Drury's Bluff with Semmes, on the James river, where he served under the command of Captain Mitchell. During this service an unsuccessful attempt was made to destroy the pontoon bridges of the Federal Army, constructed lower down the river. Soon after this Kell was invalided, after having remained some time in hospital. From that time he remained unfit for service, up to the surrender of the Army of North Virginia.

# CHAPTER 9

## FLORIDA SUNK, SHENANDOAH SAILS ON

### The *Florida*'s last prizes

After leaving Brest on 12 February 1864, Morris had first headed south, putting in at Funchal, Madeira, for supplies. Getting a poor reception there, he made for Teneriffe, where he managed to obtain all the coal and fresh supplies he needed. After leaving the island Morris cruised for about 20 days, but failed to find a Federal merchant ship until 29 March, when he sighted the full-rigged American ship *Avon*, owned by Peabody & Company of Boston. The officers and crew were taken off together with all valuables, and the unfortunate vessel used as target practice. Following the procedure now set by Confederate cruisers, Morris then pressed some of the *Avon* crew into signing for Confederacy service. It was after this incident that the *Florida* touched at St Pierre, Martinique.

The arrival of the Confederate vessel at St Pierre on 26 April prompted the local British consul, William Lawless, to write directly to Earl Russell, informing him that the vessel was carrying eight guns, and had a crew of 123 men composed principally of Italians, Austrians, and Greeks, with a few French, English and American sailors, mostly volunteers from captured vessels. A large number of these men had come ashore, and were being disorderly in their conduct. Despite their behaviour, Lawless did managed to obtain some information from them, namely that the raider had captured just one vessel since leaving Teneriffe, which had been on her way from the Chincha Islands to New York with a load of guano. Her crew, with the exception of four men put on board a vessel bound for London, had joined the *Florida*. Lawless closed by stating that the *Florida*'s presence was known to Vice-Admiral Hope, as the raider was in the roadstead when the *Duncan* had passed before the port.(1)

When the *Florida* sailed from Martinique on 7 May, steering west, it was generally supposed that she was heading towards the course usually taken by vessels bound from America to the West Indies. She left behind at St Pierre two sick officers and about six men who had deserted the ship and evaded capture by the local police, activated by Morris. Had it not been for the aid given by the authorities to secure the apprehension of deserters Lawless was convinced that a much larger number of the crew would have been left on the island. Apart from Vice Admiral Sir James Hope, the French were now also keeping a watchful eye on the Confederate vessel, one of their war steamers being positioned near the *Florida* all the time she was at St Pierre.(2)

News about the *Florida's* visit to Martinique was now getting about, and it was not long before the matter was reported to the commander of the American West Indian Squadron, Admiral James Lardner, who spent the remainder of May cruising round the local islands searching for the *Florida*. The search was fruitless, because on leaving Martinique Morris had taken his ship directly to Bermuda, where he arrived on Saturday 18 June. Here he asked for permission to take on coals, and also to have some repair work undertaken – at Her Majesty's dockyard. The latter request was immediately transmitted to Vice-Admiral Sir James Hope, who declined to allow any repair work to be carried out but did Morris a favour by sending officers on board the *Florida* to ascertain the extent of repairs necessary. Coals were then taken on board, without formal permission from the Acting Governor, William Munro, who promptly reported the matter to London.(3) Charles Francis Adams later complained bitterly about this breach of British neutrality laws to Earl Russell.(4)

Captain Morris was soon off again, and while cruising near Bermuda on 1 July he captured the barque *Harriet Stevens* of New York, which was promptly destroyed, after many valuable items were taken off her. Seven days later Morris captured the whaling barque *Golconda* of New York, which was loaded with almost 2,000 barrels of whale oil. After the removal of a few supplies she was put to the torch. On 9 July he captured the schooner *Margaret Y. Davis*. The following day he struck again, when he took the *General Barry* of Maine, which was taking hay to Fortress Munro. A few hours later the *Florida* drew alongside the barque *Zelinda*, which was promptly destroyed. This high level of activity resulted from the fact that the *Florida* had now reached American coastal waters, amd was only about 40 miles from the shores of Maryland. It was whilst Morris was in this area on 10 July, and just 30 miles from the Capes of the Delaware, that he captured the US mail steamer *Electric Spark*, bound from New York for New Orleans. She was scuttled, after her crew and passengers had been put on board a passing English ship. Morris then crossed the ocean heading back to Teneriffe, where he arrived in August, taking on fresh supplies, and 150 tons of coal at Santa Cruz, without running into any problems. He then headed back towards Brazil, capturing numerous vessels en route: *B.F. Hoxie*, *Cairaissance*, *David Lapsley*, *Estelle*, *George Latimer*, *Southern Rights*, *Greenland*, *Windward* and the *William C. Clarke*.(5)

## An ignoble end

The Confederate commander then made the greatest mistake of his career by taking his ship into Bahia, where he arrived at 9am on 4 October 1864. Here he found in port the United States steam corvette *Wachusett*, which was under the command of Captain Napoleon Collins. The United States commander, unable to believe his good luck, at once decided that – despite problems presented by his obligation to observe the neutra-

*Confederate Cruiser 'Shenandoah'*

lity of Bahia – the *Florida* could not be allowed to continue her destructive cruise.

Forgetting the old maxim that all is fair in love and war, and relying implicitly upon the protection of a neutral power, Morris naively drew the loads from his guns, and gave a large proportion of his crew shore leave. On the night of 6 October, Morris, some of his officers, and about 60 members of his crew went on shore for a heavy drinking session, leaving the ship in the charge of Lieutenant Thomas K. Porter and the remainder of the

crew – all of whom were in a drunken and sleepy condition, following their shore leave.

In this condition the *Florida* was a proverbial 'sitting duck'- too great a temptation for Commander Napoleon Collins. Notwithstanding the fact that the local American consul had just given a promise to the Governor that no hostile act towards the *Florida* by the *Wachusett* would occur in Brazilian waters, Collins decided to put diplomatic considerations on one side and take the *Florida*.

By 3am on 7th Morris and his drunken crew had still not returned to the *Florida*. Quietly, Collins gave the order to his crew to slip the moorings, and his man-of-war first moved slowly round the bay, then headed directly for the stern of the *Florida*, running into her and carrying away the raider's mizenmast. At the same time, the crew of the *Wachusett* discharged grape-shot from the forecastle gun and musketry along the deck of the *Florida* – calling for her to surrender. The firing was kept up for some time until Lieutenant Porter decided he had had enough, and complied with the demand to surrender.

The boats from the *Wachusett* then came alongside and took possession of the *Florida*, slipping her cable, making a hawser fast around the foremast of the *Wachusett*, and proceeding out of the harbour with the *Florida* in tow. Watching all of this, a Brazilian war ship which had threatened to sink the *Wachusett* if the *Florida* was attacked in the event took no action. As the *Florida* was being towed out of Bahia the fort fired three blank cartridges as an alarm, and the corvette *De Januaria* fired a few shots at the *Wachusett* as she steamed away with her prize. The Brazilian war-steamer *Paracusa* then got up steam as soon as she could, and with the *De Januaria* in tow set off after the *Wachusett*, but after an unsuccessful cruise of about five hours they gave up the chase and returned to port.(6) The *Florida* was then taken to Hampton Roads, where she was sunk, according to the official declaration of the United States Government, through ''an unforseen accident'', after a collision with an army transport.

There can be no doubt that the capture of the *Florida* was a gross and deliberate violation of the rights of a neutral nation. Although it was the independent act of an officer and was disavowed by the Federal Government, needless to say Collins was hailed as a hero throughout the United States. The infamous Confederate raider *Florida* was sunk at last, and the average man in the street knew little, and cared less, about international legal considerations.(7)

After the capture of the *Florida* Captain Morris and Taylor, his purser, were taken to Southampton by the *Magdalena*, and the remaining officers and men of the *Florida* who had been ashore at Bahia made their way to London on an English sailing ship. The crew who were with the *Florida* when she was sunk were put in prison in Washington.(8)

## A hero's welcome

Interestingly, these men in fact arrived at Boston, bound for Washington Prison, by way of the *Kearsage*! After sinking the *Alabama*, Captain Winslow had been ordered to go in hot pursuit of the *Florida*, but had soon been relieved by other United States ships, notably the *Niagara* and the *Sacramento*. The victor of the *Alabama* therefore set sail for home. On 29 October the battle-scarred *Kearsage* touched at St Thomas, and whilst replenishing her coal supplies the *Wachusett*, accompanied by the

*Florida*, came in. Collins transferred his prisoners to Winslow's ship to avoid over-crowding, and so the *Kearsage* set sail for Boston.

Winslow's welcome at Boston was overwhelmimg, for apart from being greeted as the victor of the *Alabama*, he was also able to announce that the notorious Confederate raider *Florida* had also been swept from the seas. A banquet was laid on for him by Boston Board of Trade, which was followed by scores of similar events up and down the country. The New York Chamber of Commerce presented him with a gift of $25,000 in recognition of his service to America. Amid wild acclaim in the United States Winslow was promoted to Commodore, effective from the date of the battle with the *Alabama*. Until the end of the war Abraham Lincoln used him at functions to stimulate the fervour of the public. Despite the loss of sight in one eye and generally poor health, the brave old mariner served as commander of the Gulf Squadron through 1866-67. Promoted to Rear Admiral on 2 March 1870, he took command of the Pacific Fleet. He was ordered home to be retired on 19 November 1872, but by a special Act of Congress he was continued on the active list. He died at Boston Highlands on 29 September 1873, survived by his wife, two sons, and a daughter.(9)

## The *Shenandoah*'s brief reign

Developments on the North American continent had meanwhile been moving to a conclusion. In October Grant had ordered General Sheridan to lay waste the great Shenandoah valley. Everthing that could be of use to the Confederacy was gathered up or destroyed. It was as desolate as though a wave of flame had swept down the beautiful valley. The North suffered heavy losses, but the Confederate forces were swept away in the ensuing decisive battle. On 8 November 1864 Lincoln was re-elected, with Andrew Johnson of Tennessee being elected Vice President on Lincoln's ticket. Lincoln was noticeably relieved by the outcome, having expressed much concern during the preceding months about a possible defeat. However, before the month was out, on 25 November, Confederate agents started 19 fires in New York in an attempt to spread a conflagration in revenge for the Shenandoah valley campaign.

It was in this hopeless situation, with the South reduced to taking rearguard action on the streets of New York, that James Dunwoody Bulloch from his base in Liverpool completed his plans to replace the *Alabama* with yet another Confederate raider. This ship left Britain as the *Sea King*, but was rapidly converted into the *Shenandoah*. It was from the decks of this vessel that the last shots were to be fired in the name of the Confederate States.

Captain James Dunwoody Bulloch first set eyes on the East Indiaman *Sea King* in the latter part of September 1863, well before he needed a replacement for the *Alabama*. He caught sight of her when he was on the Clyde, trying to buy a blockade runner for a specific mission. She was a fine full-rigged ship, fitted with a powerful engine and, importantly, a device for lifting her screw so that she could proceed under sail alone without the screw acting as a drag and impeding her progress through the water. Bulloch took details of the ship, and noted that she was then bound for Bombay on her maiden voyage, but would probably be back in eight to ten months time. To his mind she seemed to be almost custom-built for the role of a Confederate raider. Furthermore, when the *Alabama* was sunk and Bulloch instructed his agents to find him a suitable replacement without delay, they reported the availability of the very ship that had impressed him some ten months earlier. He immediately purchased her on behalf of the Confederacy for the sum of £45,000, through the medium of an English merchant captain named Corbett, who was to transfer her on the high seas. At the same time he purchased the blockade-runner *Laurel*, and loaded her at Liverpool with guns, stores etc for the cruiser.

Bulloch gave command of the *Shenandoah* to Captain James Iredell Waddell who, like Bulloch, had been on active service in the Mexican War. He had been promoted to the rank of Lieutenant on 15 September 1855, after which he went on a voyage to Central America. For a while he taught navigation in the Naval Academy, but then went on a tour of duty to the Orient. When he returned in 1862 he resigned due to his sympathy for the Confederacy, and his name was stricken from the rolls on 18 January 1862. He secretly entered the Confederacy through Baltimore, and was commissioned a lieu-

tenant in the Confederate States Navy on 27 March 1862.

Waddell then saw Farragut's fleet capture New Orleans. A few weeks later he served with the Drewry's Bluff Batteries in the repulse of the James River Flotilla supporting McClellan's peninsular campaign. Similar battery duty at Charleston until March 1863 ended his service within the Confederacy. He was then sent to Paris for duty under the general direction of Captain James Dunwoody Bulloch, who subsequently brought him to Liverpool to serve as commander of the *Shenandoah*.(10)

Charles Francis Adams was soon abreast of the new developments and wrote to Earl Russell, outlining the sequence of events relating to the *Sea King* and the *Laurel*. He noted that on 8 October 1864 a steamer had been dispatched under the British flag from London, called the *Sea King*, with a view to meeting another steamer, the *Laurel*, which bore the same flag and had left Liverpool on 9 October, at some point near the island of Madeira. Of concern to Adams was the fact that at the time of sailing both ships were manned by British subjects, and they were sent out with arms and enlisted men for the clear purpose of ''initiating a hostile enterprise to the people of the United States, with whom Great Britain was at the time under solemn obligation to preserve the peace.''(11) The *Laurel* had in fact left Liverpool, ostensibly as a passenger ship with general cargo bound for Havana, under the command of Captain Ramsay who, notwithstanding his British Board of Trade Master Mariner's Ticket, was a lieutenant in the Confederate Navy. Sailing with this Confederate officer were men who had actually served on the *Alabama* and who knew exactly what would later be expected of them, but the majority of the crew had signed on the understanding that they were on a normal voyage to the Far East.

One of the crew was John Ellison, who later described what happened on the *Sea King* after leaving British waters. Ellison, who signed on as Quartermaster of the *Sea King*, reported that after several days at sea they came to Madeira, where the ship went into the bay and was joined the following morning by the *Laurel*. The two vessels made their way together to the shores of a nearby uninhabited island called Las Desertas. One of the 'passengers' now stated that he was the real Captain of the ship, and ordered Corbett to hoist the Confederate flag. Captain Corbett called all the men together, informing them that he had just sold the ship – and that "This gentleman is offering £4 for ordinary seamen". At this, John Ellison told Corbett that he had broken his agreement, which was that they were to proceed to Bombay; he explained that he was an English seaman and as such was not prepared to serve the Confederacy. Corbett increased the cash offered, but with little success, only a few men agreeing to sign up. Faced with this situation the ship was then taken to Tenerife, where they arrived on 20 October, although those not wishing to serve the Confederacy were not allowed to land until 22nd.(12) In all, only about 23 men had come forward, who included the *Alabama* men, some of whom were at once promoted to warrant rank. Waddell was demoralised by this poor showing and almost tempted to call off the cruise, but eventually decided to continue. The ship was well armed, all the required guns, ammunition and so on having been transferred from the tender to the cruiser whilst at the island of Las Desertas.

Waddell was under orders to concentrate upon the untouched New England whaling fleets in the Pacific, so promptly set sail for Australia. Before arriving at Melbourne on 25 January 1865, he made prizes of the barques *Alina*, *Godfrey*, *Edward*, and *Delphine*; the schooners *Charles Oak* and *Lizzie M. Stacey*; and the brig *Susan*, all of which were burned. In addition, the steamer *Kate Prince* was ransomed to take the prisoners home.

The arrival of the *Shenandoah* at Melbourne was duly noted by Blanchard, the United States consul, who wrote to the Governor, Sir C. Darling on 27 January, objecting to repair and servicing facilities being made available to the Confederate ship.(13) The *Melbourne Argus* also noted the arrival of the vessel, informing its readers about the ships destroyed by Waddell on the way to Melbourne and the fact that Waddell was most anxious to get his ship to sea once again, quoting from one of the letters which he had addressed to the government:

"I am extremely anxious to get the *Shenandoah* to sea. The procrastination by the parties employed under his Excellency the Governor's permission for the necessary repairs to this ship seem to me unnecessary; and if I appeal to his excellency the governor for further instructions to those employed to hurry up the work on this ship, I hope his Excellency the Governor will see in it the spirit of a law-abiding man, and one impatient to be about his country's business.''(14)

The ''law-abiding'' Waddell left Melbourne in the *Shenandoah* soon after this letter was published, and proceeded under sail to the proposed cruising grounds in the neighbourhood of the Behring Straits. Here he captured and burned a large number of whalers. On one occasion eight prizes were taken together, as they gathered around the disabled ship *Brunswick*. This occurred on 28 June near the mouth of the Behring Straits, and comprised the last war exploit of the *Shenandoah* – in a war which had actually already ended! In fact, many of the captures of the *Shenandoah* were made after the close of the war, prompting Secretary Welles to accuse Waddell of continuing his belligerent operations when he knew that the armies of the South had surrendered. However, it seems clear that Waddell was out of touch with the situation in America, for from prizes taken on 23 June he obtained papers relating to the preceding April which covered Lee's surrender to Grant, the Confederate government's removal from Richmond to Danville, and Jefferson Davis' proclamation stating that the fight would continue.

At long last, however, the *Shenandoah* came out of the Straits on 29 June, and while running towards the California coast spoke, on 2 August, to the British barque *Baracouta*, fourteen days out of San Fran-

cisco.(15) The Captain of this ship finally managed to convince Waddell that the Confederacy had indeed collapsed. When this sank in Waddell faced reality: he disarmed the ship and crew, the boiler fires were put out, and the carpenters put to work closing the gun ports. After some discussion it was eventually decided that they should make their way back to Liverpool, in spite of the long run of 17,000 miles around Cape Horn; this run was made without sighting land, or exchanging signals with another ship. With her Confederate flag flying, the *Shenandoah* eventually sailed up the Mersey on 5 November 1865.(16) Whilst Waddell had been on this last cruise, for all the world like some seagoing Rip Van Winkle, much had indeed taken place in America, which was reflected in activity on Merseyside.

# CHAPTER 10

## THE FINAL MONTHS OF THE CONFEDERACY

### The last Confederate ships

The year 1865 opened with every prospect of a speedy end to the Civil War. Sherman's march to the sea had rent the dying Confederacy even more disastrously than the opening of the Mississippi which had previously split it into two large fragments. Everywhere, the Union forces had been victorious. By 1 February Sherman was on his way north through the Carolinas with 60,000 men, and on 27th Sheridan was able to start up the Shenandoah valley again with 10,000 cavalry.

The Confederates were on the run, but this did nothing to prevent pro-Confederacy activity continuing unabated on Merseyside; Messrs Jones, Quiggin & Company, shipbuilders of Sefton Street, were notable in their efforts to launch blockade-runners efficiently, and thus give support to the dying beast. On 25 February the London press reported that on the previous Wednesday a most unusual event was witnessed by a huge crowd at the Jones, Quiggin yard – namely the simultaneous launch of five steamers. One of these, the *Noor-el-Huda*, had been built for an Egyptian company and was intended for Red Sea work, but the others were built for anonymous owners and were clearly designed as blockade-runners. These four were the *Widgeon*, *Curlew*, *Plover* and *Snipe* – all fast paddle steamers, 225 feet long, with shallow holds 11 feet deep. The reporter concluded his piece: ''For whom these steamers have been built we were not informed; but from their general appearance, there can be little doubt that they are intended for some service in connection with the running of the blockade of the Southern ports.''(1)

Blockade running had undoubtedly lined the pockets of many Liverpool shipowners and merchants during the civil war and, as late as September 1863, 23 vessels were employed in ''keeping up communication'' between Wilmington and other Confederate ports. (2) A typical pro-Confederacy, pro-blockade running comment being:

''But Liverpool shipowners did not sit down quietly and lament this sudden and unexpected blow, (The blockade cutting off supplies of cotton) it had never been their way, and almost from the first they were up and doing. Britain was a neutral nation, it is true, but the merchants and seamen of this great northern port maintained that it was not a crime to attempt to run a foreign blockade; nor was it a breach of neutrality. Those days of the 'sixties were glorious days at sea, and Liverpool was full of hardy seamen who had been trained in the beautiful sailing craft of that era. Stout-hearted sailors they were, imbued with the sp;irit of adventure.'' (3) Those who refused to sail for the Confederacy, or were fighting on the battlefields of North America, to end slavery, no doubt seeing the activities of these merchants, and ''stout hearted'' adventurers, in those ''Glorious Days'' in a somewhat different light!

Confederate plans to obtain armed men-of-war on Merseyside had been frustrated when the infamous Laird Rams were impounded, but this had led to the Confederate agents attempting to obtain similar vessels from France – efforts which were stopped by the timely intervention of the French Government. Six vessels of this type were built, but only one, the *Stonewall*, found its way to the Confederacy, and this was only in 1865 when the war was almost over. She was a formidable looking vessel, with a ram bow, heavy armaments, and armoured sides some 5 inches thick. This lumbering beast made her way to Ferrol in March, 1865, and fell in with the United States frigate *Niagara* and the sloop-of-war *Sacramento*, who took up positions in the adjoining port of Coruna. Eventually the *Stonewall* made her way out of the harbour of Coruna, and gave some indication that she would welcome taking on the Federal ships. The *Niagara* and *Sacramento* refrained from attacking her, knowing that an engagement with this vessel would have ended disastrously. Unmolested, the *Stonewall* made her way to Lisbon and then to Havana, where she was surrendered to the United States by the Spanish Government,

the war having terminated. She was subsequently sold to Japan.(2)

## Surrender

On 4 March, 1865, Abraham Lincoln had taken office for the second time as President of the United States. There was one new and striking feature in the simple ceremony, the presence of a battalion of negro troops in his escort – the historical significance of which cannot be underestimated.(3) The President, looking tired, delivered his speech in a high, almost unbroken voice. He said that no one could have expected the cause of the war to cease before the conflict itself had ceased, but that slavery, nevertheless, had perished. He continued by saying that if it were God's will, the country must see this war through to a conclusion, ''with malice towards none; with charity for all... to do all which may achieve a just, and lasting peace, among ourselves, and with all nations.''(4)

Just over one month after Lincoln had spoken these words, on Thursday 6 April, the Confederate General Robert E. Lee lost 7,000 men at Sailors's Creek, mostly as prisoners. Grant, now feeling that his hold on Lee could not be shaken, wrote him a letter on the Friday afternoon, saying ''The result of the last week must convince you of the hopelessness of further resistance.'' That night Lee replied asking what terms Grant proposed to offer. Next morning Grant wrote again proposing a meeting, and Lee wrote to say he was willing to treat for peace.(5) On 9 April 1865 the two generals met in the Court House at Appomattox, Virginia, and

Lee surrendered the Army of Northern Virginia, thus effectively ending the American Civil War.

Just before this, and as soon as he heard that Richmond had fallen, Lincoln had made his way to the city that had been occupied by the fallen Confederate Congress. Here he walked unattended, except for a boat's crew, and leading his small child by the hand. Those who witnessed the event stated that he walked like a man in a dream. Within moments he was surrounded by thousands of black people -liberated slaves, the only people left in the city. They welcomed him as the great Liberator: they shouted, cheered, danced, then prayed for him and many fell to the ground weeping, and kneeling at his feet.(6) Perhaps the most dramatic moment of all came when an old black man recognised Lincoln, and cried out: "I knew him as soon as I saw him. He's been in my heart for long years. Glory Hallelujah!" With this he fell to his knees. But Lincoln told him: "Don't kneel for me. You must kneel to God only and thank Him for your freedom." (7)

The tears streamed down Lincoln's face as he continued on his way through the city. For a while, speechless with emotion, he simply bowed his thanks, or raised his hat to the jubilant and almost hysterical mass of liberated slaves. After a while he arrived at Jefferson Davis's former headquarters. When an officer here suggested to him that Davis should be hanged, characteristically Lincoln replied gently: "Judge not, that ye be not judged."

The President then hurried back to visit Seward, who had suffered injuries in a fall from his carriage. It was that night, 9 April, that Lincoln received a telegram from Grant which simply stated: "General Lee surrendered the army of Northern Virginia this morning on terms proposed by myself." Lincoln, victorious at last, later spoke to a vast crowd on the White House lawn. He showed no trace of triumph. He was concerned only with laying the foundations of a lasting peace.

## The death of Lincoln

North and South had scarcely grasped the full significance of Lee's surrender when, only five days later, Lincoln was assassinated. "It would be impossible for me," said Grant, "to describe the feeling that overcame me at the news. I knew his goodness of heart, and above all his desire to see all the people of the United States enter upon the full privileges of citizenship with equality among all." America was stunned by the news.

On Wednesday 19 April, the funeral of the dead president took place at the White House. Thousands of men, women, and children passed through the building to take their last look at the face of Lincoln, white in his coffin. It was a memorable spectacle, the weeping and crying attesting to the genuine grief of those who crowded the White House to see the Emancipator for the last time. A politician of immense stature was dead, but the words of Stanton, his Secretary of State for War, spoken at the

time of his death, summed up the feelings of millions: "Now he belongs to the ages."

There then followed an unprecedented demonstration of grief in America. Lincoln was buried in Oak Ridge Cemetary, Illinois. The funeral train left Washington on 21 April, and traversed nearly the same route that had been passed over by the train that bore him, President-elect, from Springfield to Washington five years before. It was a unique funeral, and utterly staggering in its proportions. The funeral train travelled almost 2,000 miles, and with the engineer driving slowly the train took hours to pass its many given points. Many millions of people saw it, moved in it and were part of its procession. People lined the entire 2,000 miles almost without an interval, standing with uncovered heads, many mute with grief, as the sombre cortège swept by. Even darkness and heavy rainfall did not deter them from the line of the procession. At night the scene became even more dramatic, with the train slowly passing hundreds of

*Ford's Theatre, Washington, where Lincoln was shot. (Tina Hollett)*

watch-fires that had been lit along the route. In some of the larger cities Lincoln's coffin was lifted gently from the funeral train and carried through the streets, followed by thousands of weeping citizens. Thus honoured in his funeral, he was guarded to his grave by famed and battle-scarred generals of the Army.

Vice-President Andrew Johnson now became President, and after much misunderstanding the surrender of the remaining Confederate armies was effected, then: "Each body of troops laid down its arms and quietly dispersed. One day the bugles called, the camp fires burned, and comrades were together in the ranks. The next, like morning mists, they disappeared, thenceforth to be remembered and admired only as the heroes of a hopeless cause."(8)

On 23 and 24 May it was a vastly different scene, when over a million men of the victorious Union forces were reviewed in Washington. The column was 30 miles long. For over six hours on each day the troops marched past, along a route flagged from end to end with Stars and Stripes and lined with thousands of cheering citizens. With bayonets flashing in the sun the long blue column flowed for hour after hour, and as they passed by the bands played and the men sang the Battle Hymn of the Republic, the sentiments of which were dedicated to the ending of slavery:

"Mine eyes have seen the glory of the coming of the Lord; He is trampling out the vintage where the grapes of wrath are stored; He has loosed the fateful lightning of his terrible swift sword; His truth is marching on. Glory, glory, hallelujah, Glory, glory, hallelujah, Glory, glory, hallelujah, His truth is marching on. I have seen him in the watchtowers of a hundred circling camps; They have builded him an altar in the evening dews and damps; I can read his righteous sentence by the dim and flaring lamps; His day is marching on. In the beauty of the lilies Christ was born across the sea; With a glory in his bosom that transfigures you and me; As he died to make men holy, let us die to make men free, While God is marching on.''

## The news reaches Liverpool

It was on Thursday 27 April that Liverpool, the town linked with the lost cause of the Confederacy, first heard that President Abraham Lincoln had been assassinated. The press gave a full account of how Lincoln had been in his private box at Ford's Theatre

*Departure of the train carrying the body of Abraham Lincoln*

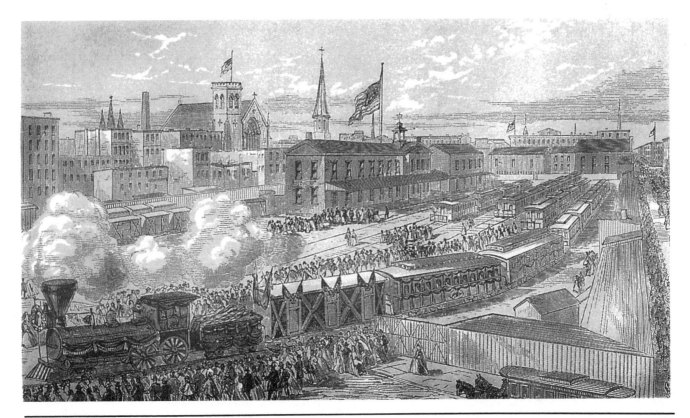

when the assassin (John Wilkes Booth – an unbalanced young actor) had gained admission to the President's box on the pretence of being the bearer of dispatches from General Grant, and then deliberately shot him from behind with a one-barrel pistol. Booth had then jumped from the box to the stage, flourishing a dagger and exclaiming *"Sic semper tyrannis!"* – the words used by Brutus when he killed Caesar, and also the motto of Virginia.(9) (Booth was later caught and killed.)

Subsequent events in Liverpool revealed that there were more people in the town sympathetic to the cause of Lincoln than to the cause of the Confederacy which had been so warmly embraced by some Liverpool merchants, shipbuilders and shipowners. On the same day, two mass meetings were called by the Mayor to express indignation and sorrow at the assassination of Abraham Lincoln. The first meeting took place in the afternoon, and was held in the huge St George's Hall. Thousands flooded in, the vast body of the hall being completed filled, and the galleries also packed from one end to the other. The platform was crowded with the leading members of the mercantile community: partisans of the South united with partisans of the North in demonstrating their indignation at this crime. Amongst those present were H. Wilding (American Vice-Consul), J.A. Tinne, of the old-established firm of Sandbache Tinne & Company, H. Littledale, John Cropper, M. Williams, Robert Trimble, John Shimmin, Thomas Earl, C.R. Hall, Doctor Graham, John Forwood, Thomas Brandon, and Isaac Cook.

The mayor addressed the huge crowd, describing how a "thrill of horror" had shot through the town when the flash of the electric telegraph conveyed the painful intelligence that President Lincoln had been ruthlessly massacred, and his Chief Secretary dangerously, if not mortally wounded. Speaker followed speaker, all condemning the crime, and many remarking on the evils of slavery, to loud clapping and cheering. After a few hours the meeting closed, and the businessmen returned to their offices.

At 7pm the second meeting was held in St George's Hall, timed to allow the working people of the town to attend. This meeting was even more densely packed than the one in the afternoon. Mr Charles Wilson presided, and amongst those present was the Reverend William Binns from Birkenhead. The chairman opened the proceedings by stating that they had met to express their horror and indignation at an awful crime, as black as any in the pages of history. He described Lincoln as the best friend the South ever had: "A far better friend than those who had led them to ruin." These observations brought loud cheering from the audience. Wilson continued to praise Lincoln: "through all these years of rebellion no one could point their finger to a word of President Lincoln, either from his pen or his lips, which showed revenge, animosity, or cruelty." It was the sting in the tail of slavery in its death throes that had killed Abraham Lincoln, and Wilson trusted they would avenge themselves upon that avowed serpent that had been his death. No Englishman wanted to see slavery live, Wilson continued, and he trusted that the blows levied against slavery (by Lincoln) would see it exterminated for ever from the land; if it was driven from America united, it would disappear from the whole world. As in the afternoon meeting, speaker after speaker rose to express horror at the criminal assassination and of slavery. The last speaker of the day was Edmund Jones, a working man, who expressed the hope that hatred and slavery would be buried together in the grave of Abraham Lincoln. Commenting on the hypocrisy of many who were now mourning the death of Lincoln, Jones stated:

''It was a sad thing to think that a man must be sacrificed before he could earn the reputation due to him [and] that public writers and speakers, who had hitherto tried to cover the immortal Abraham Lincoln with everything derogatory to dignity, unworthy the head of a might people – it was strange to observe that certain individuals who a short time ago pronounced Abraham Lincoln the illiterate backwoodsman and buffoon,

*St Georges Hall, Liverpool, ca. 1900; this was the scene of two mass meetings on 27th April 1865 called to express indignation and sorrow at the assassination of Abraham Lincoln.*

and denounced him as the ignorant Joe Miller, should that day placard the walls of this town, and tell the public, with grave mockery, humility, and apparent sorrow, that they were prepared to furnish the interesting details of the life of Abraham Lincoln.''

These observations brought loud cries of applause and laughter, as Jones continued that he had felt justified in concluding that this mock sympathy was to be calculated by pence shillings and pounds – but the sympathy of his fellow working men was genuine and sincere. After a further resolution, the meeting came to an end.(9)

## Reaction in America

In America, the full implications of Lincoln's death were sinking in. Former slaves were particularly shocked at the assassination of the President, for to them Lincoln represented the end of slavery and hope for the future. The war was over, and slavery had been abolished by the Thirteenth Amendment of the Constitution; but would the white people of the South really accept the new situation, particularly without Abraham Lincoln to guide the nation through the difficult period that lay ahead? A letter written by a Negro poet, F.E.W. Harper a few days after the death of Lincoln, shows both hope and apprehension:

''Sorrow treads on the footsteps of the nation's joy. A few days since the telegraph thrilled and throbbed the nation's joy. Today a nation sits down beneath the shadow of its mournful grief. Oh what a terrible lesson does this event read to us!... Well, it may be in the providence of God this blow was needed to intensify the nation's hatred of slavery, to show the utter fallacy of basing national reconstruction upon the votes of returned rebels, and rejecting loyal black men....Moses, the meekest man on earth, led the children of Israel over the Red Sea, but was not permitted to see them settle in Canaan. Mr Lincoln has led [us] up through another Red Sea to the table land of Triumphant victory, and God has seen fit to summon for the new era another man....Let the whole nation resolve that the whole virus shall be eliminated from its body; that in the future slavery shall only be remembered as a thing of the past that shall never have the faintest hope of resurrection.''

For ten days after killing Lincoln, John Wilkes Booth was on the run, managing to avoid thousands of Union soldiers and police officers as he fled from Washington to Maryland and then over to Virginia. Eventually he crossed the Rappahannock river and went into hiding on Richard Garrett's farm. The barn he was in was surrounded by troops, and when Booth refused to surrender the soldiers set fire to the building. A few moments passed, and then a shot rang out. Five hours later Booth died of the wound, coincidentally at the same hour as the great man he had murdered.

On 10 May Jefferson Davis was captured near Irwinville, Georgia. His wife and other members of the Confederate Government were also taken into custody. When captured, Davis, the man who had led the Rebellion, was disguised as a woman. He had become a political and military leader after graduation from West Point, but soon one of his best generals, Pierre Beauregard, joined with other detractors and claimed that the South was slowly nibbled away, not crushed, ''because its executive head never gathered and wielded its great strength.''

# CHAPTER 11

## THE AFTERMATH OF THE CIVIL WAR

### Politics in Birkenhead

Back in Birkenhead in May 1865 John Laird, the small town politician, was about to stand for election once more, in a town economically dominated by the great Laird family shipbuilding enterprise.

Spring 1865 had been a traumatic period in the history of America. It was also, on a local scale, a notable time in the life of John Laird, his sons, and their workers at Birkenhead. At about the same time that Lairds had accepted the contract from Bulloch to build the *Alabama*, work was also started on another vessel, the 6,621-ton man-of-war HMS *Agincourt*. Though the *Alabama* had been given the yard number 290 and HMS *Agincourt* number 291, it was to be almost three years after the launch of the Confederate vessel before work on the *Agincourt* was completed. Work on the ship continued during the remaining period of the American Civil War, with which John Laird had become so deeply involved.

The launch of the *Agincourt* took place on 27 March 1865 in the presence of about 30,000 suitably impressed spectators. They crowded every available vantage point in order to witness the undocking of the largest ship ever to be built at Birkenhead. The immense hull of the *Agincourt* was slowly but surely undocked with the assistance of six powerful steam tugs, and as she emerged from the dock there was a thundering salute of 21 guns from Laird's own company of Artillery Volunteers. The huge crowd were wild with patriotic excitement as one of the most powerful vessels of war ever constructed entered the Mersey.(1)

In the evening Laird Brothers celebrated the successful floating of the huge vessel by entertaining their managers of departments, clerks, foremen, and a few friends, at the Monks Ferry Hotel – a company in all numbering about 150. After the meal the usual toasts were made, perhaps the most significant one being made by H.K. Aspinall, who proposed "The town and trade of Birkenhead"; he declared that Birkenhead was now represented by an excellent Member in Parliament, and at the next election they would take care to send that gentleman back to represent them again. After appropriate cheers, Aspinall concluded by applauding the benefits derived by Birkenhead from the works of Messrs Laird, and hoping that they would obtain more orders from the Government and the commercial world, for ships meant more wages and – as a Mr Bold interjected – "More beer!"(2) The point had been made: vote for John Laird, as this meant work and wages for the huge percentage of Birkenhead residents employed, directly or indirectly, by the Laird family yard. As a Member of Parliament, Laird would doubtless be favoured with Government orders, despite the embarrassment caused by the *Alabama* Affair. Regarding the election, the timing of the *Agincourt* undocking and celebrations could not have been better, as it had made John Laird something of a local hero. It was no doubt because of this that the Liberal candidate, Henry Jackson, played down the *Alabama* Affair at this election – unlike the local press, who continued to pursue the controversial subject.

The Liberal candidate in the Birkenhead election was Henry Mather Jackson, the son of William Jackson MP -who, together with John Laird, was considered to be one of the founding fathers of Birkenhead. The Jackson family had moved out of the area by this time, William being the MP for Newcastle under Lyme; and at this election William Jackson had taken his leave of the electors of Newcastle to standing as Liberal candidate for North Derbyshire.

The extension of the franchise was one of the big issues in this election, and the first shot against the Liberals was fired by the *Birkenhead Advertiser* early in May.(3) The comments, ostensibly directed against William Jackson, were clearly meant to undermine the credibility of Liberals in general and Henry Mather Jackson in particular. The reporter drew attention to the fact that William Jackson had "In a manner befitting a Knight of the Shire" modulated his reforming zeal, and abandoned his oft-expressed desire for the immediate and wholesale enfranchisement of the masses. He

now seemed to be convinced that mere numbers could not be taken as an argument, which seemed remarkably like the Tory line!(3)

The pitch was now suitably queered for Henry Mather Jackson on this central issue, as he held the first public meeting of his 'friends and supporters' in the Theatre Royal, Argyle Street, Birkenhead on 1 June. Jackson was polite in his references to Laird as a person, pointing out that the issue was who governed the country; and he declared that he would not mention the question of the *Alabama*.(4)

On 10 June the Birkenhead press did take up the *Alabama* Affair, but in a defensive way. Its editorial column took the line that had President Lincoln been alive he would have removed all sources of "disquietude to foreign nations; but President Johnson, by the policy he has adopted, makes us reflect now and again on the oft-repeated assertion during the late war, that the South were fighting our battles, and we now see that claims of a peculiar annoying nature are about to be raised for an indemnity for the destructive ravages of our Birkenhead emissary, the *Alabama*." Clearly angered by President Johnson's decision to seek compensation from Britain for the damage done to United States shipping by the Birkenhead "emissary", the reporter took refuge behind the flimsy legal argument that "What injury the *Alabama* and other Confederate cruisers may have caused, international law exonerates us."(5)

On the same day that these comments were published, Jackson issued his election address, but made no mention of the *Alabama* Affair, making it clear that he considered the main issue at this election to be the extension of the suffrage. Jackson was obviously afraid to take the *Alabama* issue up, or was hoping for a polite campaign. But Laird supporters were now being less than polite, one scrawling on a wall "To Hell with Jackson" whereupon a Jackson supporter wrote underneath "For such love we scarcely were prepared, show me a man who would go half as far with Laird."(7)

However, the issue of the American Civil War kept surfacing during the Birkenhead election campaign. On 6 June a well attended meeting was held in the Music Hall to establish a movement to raise relief for the four million emancipated slaves in America. William Hind presided, and two Americans, Dr Storrs of Cincinnati and Leigh of New York, were prominent amongst the speakers. After Hind had declared that nothing of a party political nature should be introduced into the discussion, Hind pointed out to the audience that more than four million of their fellow creatures, differing only in the colour of their skin, had been emancipated. The almost instantaneous change in condition of 4 million people was a momentous step, and could only be brought about by the sympathy and assistance of those who felt interested in making the slaves into free men. The American visitors then gave those present a detailed account of the problems facing the emancipated slaves, and the United States Government in rebuilding the nation.

Interestingly, there is no mention of the Liberal candidate attending this meeting, and perhaps understandably John Laird MP did not attend. However, he did send a contribution of £20, with a very remarkable letter, which was read out to the audience:

"To William Hind Esq

"Birkenhead, 6 June 1865

"My Dear Sir, I regret that other engagements will prevent me attending the meeting at which you are to take the chair tonight, for the purpose of aiding the efforts now being made in America to raise funds for the relief and mental and bodily elevation of the emancipated slaves of that country.

"I understand you to say distinctly that the objects of the society are not at all political, but merely for the purpose above stated. I shall therefore have much pleasure in giving a donation towards the funds of the society.

"I may perhaps be allowed to state that my interest in the object of the meeting is greatly increased from the circumstances that my late brother, Macgregor Laird, was one of the principal originators of the first African expedition in 1832 (which he accompanied personally), and that from the period of his return until his death, a few years ago, he was one of the warmest and most energetic supporters of all proposals for the improvement and advancement of the African race in all parts of the world. Yours faithfully.

"John Laird"(8)

John Laird had given a true account of his

brother's concern for Africans, as Macgregor Laird had been a life-long opponent of the slave trade from Africa, and on two occasions had given evidence before Parliamentary Committees on how best to end the slave trade. Had he not died on 27 January 1861, before his family accepted contracts to build ships from the Confederacy, there can be no doubt that he would have opposed such involvement with a regime dedicated to the perpetuation of slavery. However, John Laird could now skilfully use his late brother's excellent record on opposition to slavery to draw attention away from his own partisan involvement with the Confederacy.

On 7 July, the Birkenhead press published in full a long letter from Richard Gaskell of Birkenhead, a leading local Liberal, which took up the *Alabama* Affair in detail. Gaskell pointed out that the '290' was intended as a Confederate cruiser, and John Laird could not have been ignorant of the fact. On the crucial question of the Foreign Enlistment Act he stated that it was intended to prevent the subjects of the Crown from going to war when the Sovereign is not at war, and that therefore private persons were prohibited from fitting out a ship of war in British ports, or from enlisting in the service of a foreign state at war with another state.

Gaskell wrote that Earl Russell had stated in a dispatch to Lord Lyons on 27 March 1863: "The *Alabama* has eluded the operations of the Foreign Enlistment Act, and has, against the will and purpose of the British Government, made war upon American commerce in the American seas." In the same dispatch he also quoted from a conversation he had with the American Ambassador: "I said the Cabinet were of the opinion that the law was sufficient, but that legal evidence could not always be procured.' That the British Government had done everything in its power to execute the law; but I admit that the case of the *Alabama* and *Oreto* were a scandal and in some degree a reproach to our laws." Gaskell continued by stating that he could give many further extracts from official papers to show that, although the parties instrumental in sending the *Alabama* to sea were not legally convicted of breaking British laws, yet in the opinion of her Majesty's Government the law had been evaded.

Gaskell continued that the great cheering for the *Alabama* reported to have taken place at Laird's election meeting should be effaced by a decided vote at the hustings, if Birkenhead was to stand blameless in the matter. He declared that no matter which political party he belonged to, he would have opposed the election of John Laird on a matter of principle. Gaskell concluded:

"When this offence has been purged by an exclusion from Parliament, till the international difficulties it has occasioned are removed, then, and not till then, should Mr Laird's friends seek to reinstate him in his former prominent position."(9)

A few days later another Laird election meeting was held, when the *Alabama* was cheered once more by wildly enthusiastic Conservative supporters. Gaskell's principled and considered arguments had fallen on deaf ears, at least so far as the limited electorate was concerned; Laird was returned once more as Member of Parliament for Birkenhead. Again in 1868, Captain Sherard Osborne, a candidate with impeccable credentials, stood for the Liberals against Laird, but was beaten – John Laird's supporters making much of the facts that Osborne was not a local man, was rather fat, and, worst of all, had once been blackballed from a London club! At the 1874 election – called at extremely short notice – a local man, James Samuelson, was put forward against Laird and stood for a variety of humanitarian causes, but Birkenhead was not ready for radicalism, and once again Laird was returned. His victories came despite the fact that, at both of these elections, Laird was reminded by his opponents of the role he had played in the American Civil War.

## Arbitration

The legality of the *Alabama* Affair was eventually settled at the Court of Arbitration at Geneva in September 1872, Count Schlopis acting as President at the Court. The arbitrators found in favour of the United States, awarding America £3,299,166 in compensation for the damage done to her shipping, notably by the *Alabama*, *Florida*, and *Shenandoah*. British law had, in fact, been tightened up after the Civil War, and it was under the new legislation that Britain consented to have the conduct of the country in respect of the British-built Confederate Raiders judged by the Court of Arbitration. The Court stated that at the time when the offences occurred, out of which the dispute arose, no such offence was known to any jurist. Although infringements of the Foreign Enlistment Act as it then stood had clearly been made, these were put on one side. But both parties agreed that offences had been committed which ought to be recognised by law, with Britain agreeing to abide by any decision the arbitrators came to.

Britain's apparently generous offer was made to avert war between the two English-speaking nations, for America had made it abundantly clear that if compensation was not made, war would follow – the loss of Canada from the British Empire being the likely outcome of any ensuing dispute. Under the circumstances, the compensation was considered a cheap sacrifice to make to cement the mutual confidence of both peoples.(10)

Needless to say, Laird took exception to the decision of the arbitrators, arguing in the House of Commons that responsibility for paying the award rested upon the Liberal Government and its Republican supporters, at whose instigation, he said, it had sacrificed the interests of the country by going into arbitration *ex post facto* and on such admissions and conditions as entitled America to a favourable verdict. All the documents had been laid before the arbitrators, "and the Messrs Laird had nothing to fear from the wild statements of itinerant orators and enthusiastic Republican members of Parliament".(11) To the last, Laird always argued about the 'legality' of the Alabama Affair, always avoiding arguments about the ethics of the issue – a convenient tradition still continued by his supporters.

# The death of John Laird

In August 1873, the year following the settlement of the 'Alabama Claims', John Laird was out riding on Bidston Hill, Birkenhead, when his horse suddenly shied at an object by the side of the road and threw its rider, who, though able to return home apparently not much the worse for the accident, was severely shaken by the fall and was confined to his bed for some days. From this point, his health deteriorated rapidly, and he died on 29 October 1874 – nine years after the conclusion of the American Civil War.

At his death, tribute was paid in the local press to the contribution he had made towards the development of Birkenhead, and his pioneering work as a great and innovative shipbuilder. Mention was also made of the fact that he was a "sound churchman" who had taken an active part in the Anti-papal aggression movement of 1851, which had provoked great riots of Catholic dock labourers when the Town Hall was besieged, its windows smashed, and several of the leading inhabitants were severely injured. John Laird had been very active in the fundamentalist Protestant movement – a grouping not renowned for religious toleration.

It was noted that when he had become a Member of Parliament he had resigned his share in the family shipbuilding firm, which had since been carried on by his three sons, William, John, and Henry H. Laird. However, in popular estimation, he had continued to be the head of the firm, and as such was looked upon as the builder of the *Alabama*, and responsible for her escape and subsequent depredations. He had sanctioned the building of two rams which almost got away, and if they had done might have broken the blockade by sweeping the seas of United States warships.

In 1863, John Bright had, in the House of Commons, criticised Laird for building the *Alabama*, and thus giving aid to a reactionary regime based on slavery. Bright was a humanitarian of great stature, who had devoted much of his time and energy to championing the cause of the poor and opposing slavery and had gained the respect of the masses, whose cause he championed. To Bright, John Laird had responded with these words:

"I would rather be handed down to posterity as the builder of a dozen *Alabamas* than as the man who applies himself deliberately to set class against class, and to cry up the institutions of another country, which, when they come to be tested are of no value whatsoever, and which reduce liberty to a mere absurdity."

Without a doubt, John Laird *has* been handed down to posterity as the builder of the *Alabama* and as the man who had worked to assist the Confederates. Bright, on the other hand, contrary to Laird's judgement, has been handed down to posterity as a supporter of the poor and downtrodden.

John Laird's oratorical abilities were never great, and he seldom made use of them in the House. However, his eminence as an iron shipbuilder, and especially as a builder

*The John Laird statue, Hamilton Square, Birkenhead. (Chris Sarson)*

of ironclad men-of-war, should have guaranteed him both a title and a Junior Lordship of the Admiralty. He was passed over because of the *Alabama* Affair, for the obvious reason that an '*Alabama* Administration' would have done nothing to help Great Britain re-establish good relations with the United States of America.

Like all controversial characters, John Laird had his supporters and detractors, which was reflected at the time of his death. Just before he died, thousands called each day to scan the bulletins outside his home which gave information about his deteriorating condition, and his health was the subject of conversation on both sides of the Mersey. When he passed away late at night the news spread quickly throughout the town he had done much to create – many expressing sympathy with the Laird family. On the Friday the flags on the Mersey ferry boats, public buildings, and several large establishments, were hoisted at half mast. The long obituary columns published in the Birkenhead press were lined with black, a custom of the day normally reserved for reporting the death of Royalty. The *Liverpool Daily Post* concluded its obituary notice:

"Perhaps not a man of brilliant parts, he was distinguished by a hard-headed acuteness which stood him in good stead throughout life, not possessed of a high class of genius he was endowed with a considerable portion of that which Carlyle holds to be its best substitute, 'a sublime capacity for taking trouble'. He was not one to lead a nation, but in a borough like Birkenhead a partisan leader of consummate ability, not a man of much breadth of thought, but of great perspicacity, quick to take hold of an idea and bold to carry it through in spite of evey obstacle, with a dogged determination which nothing could daunt, no difficulty dismay. Such men rise to power in circumstances like those in which Birkenhead has hitherto been placed, and in the conduct of local affairs they find their natural field of operations, and are enabled to take a position which circumstances might never offer them on a wider scale.''(12)

In short, John Laird was a local businessman and conservative politician, with a limited understanding of issues outside his sphere of activity. He was completely out of his depth on national and international issues, or when attempting to make a correct evaluation of the major issues of his day. But his limitations were common ones; his views representative of many of his class and party in the nineteenth century.

## The fate of the Confederates

As for Raphael Semmes, when the Confederates surrendered at Greensboro he was captured and placed on parole, on 1 May 1865. He made his was back to his home in Mobile, where he was arrested (on 15 December 1865) by order of the Secretary of the Navy. He was taken prisoner to Washington where he was held for three months. The charge was that he had violated the usages of war in escaping from the *Alabama* after her colours had been struck. He was held for trial before a military commission, but the Supreme Court denied the jurisdiction of these commissions and he was released by Presidential order. Upon his return home he was elected probate judge of Mobile County on 7 May 1866, but was driven out of office by military force under orders from the Secretary of War.

The philosophy that had given birth to the Confederacy did not die with the surrender of the South – men like Semmes being, if anything, more popular than ever amongst the reactionaries of the Deep South after surrender. It is not therefore surprising that upon his return home Semmes was offered another influential post – the chair of moral philosophy and English literature at Louisiana State Seminary – in the autumn of 1866. Once again, however, this proved too much for his opponents, and he was forced out of the professorship by political pressure before the end of the school year.

The multi-talented sea captain then turned his hand to journalism. He became the editor of the *Memphis Daily Bulletin*, which gave him another opportunity to propagate his brand of moral philosophy. Again, those with a more progressive outlook succeeded in flushing him out of his employment. Undaunted, Semmes found another way of spreading the word and making a living by embarking on a profitable lecture tour of the States. After this venture he returned to Mobile, where he practised law until his death on 30 August 1877 at his home on Point Clear, Mobile Bay. He was buried the next day in the Catholic graveyard, Mobile, with full public honours and much mourning.(13)

Although Raphael Semmes managed to evade imprisonment after the collapse of the South, his leader Jefferson Davis was not so fortunate. The news of Lee's surrender prompted Davis to flee to the south. On 12 April at Greensboro, a cabinet meeting was held which Beauregard and Johnston attended. Davis gave Johnston permission to negotiate the surrender of his army to Sherman. Twelve days later, at Charlotte, Jefferson Davis held his last cabinet meeting, which approved Johnston's surrender – and belatedly acknowledged that the Confederacy had been defeated. Davis then continued to flee south, hoping to evade capture and make his way out of the country. But the Federal cavalry were in hot pursuit, and managed to capture him on 10 May 1865 at Irwinville.

Davis spent the next two years as a prisoner in Fortress Monroe, held for much of the time in irons on the instructions of Assistant Secretary of War, Charles A. Dana. His health began to fail, at which point he was assigned to comfortable quarters, which his family were permitted to share. Attempts were then made to bring him to trial, but the lawyers employed by the Federal government detected technical flaws in all the charges that were suggested. He was eventually released on bond on 13 May 1867, and although he had lost his fortune and his home, cash was found to enable him to make a tour of Europe.

Davis then tried his hand at various business ventures which failed. Though a portion of his Briarfield estate was saved, he ended his days as a poor man. A home was provided for his old age through the bequest of Mrs Sarah A. Dorsey, a friend of Mrs Davis, at 'Beauvoir' on the Gulf of Mexico. Here he spent the three years 1878-81, writing his own lengthy account of the Civil War, in which he expanded on the essential 'justice' of his lost cause. Though the state of Mississippi would willingly have sent him to the Senate, he could not bring himself to ask for the Federal pardon without which it was impossible for him to take his seat. He died at New Orleans on 6 December 1889 in his eighty-second year.(14)

Captain James Dunwoody Bulloch, Confederate agent in Liverpool, managed to evade a term of imprisonment in the United States. This he achieved by spending the remainder of his life in Liverpool. Here he earned a living by establishing various small ventures, out of which he made very little money. Under the chairmanship of his son-in-law, Alderman M. Hyslop Maxwell, he sat on the committee of the Liverpool Nautical College and also, to his credit, took an active interest in the Orphan Boy's Asylum, Myrtle Street.

On 7 January 1901 the Liverpool press announced the death of Agnes Macgregor Laird,(15) the daughter of John Laird, who had been been given her uncle's name. Ironically, two days later, the same paper announced the death of Captain James Dunwoody Bulloch. The small obituary notice in the *Liverpool Mercury* regarding James Dunwoody Bulloch concluded that "While representing the Confederates it is stated that he disbursed millions, and finally left himself penniless, thus setting an example which American public servants have by no means invariably followed.''(16) Whilst it is clear from this that Bulloch did not take advantage of his position of trust with the Confederacy to enrich himself, he did not die entirely penniless. At the time of his death on January 7 1901, he was living in Canning Street, Liverpool with Martha Louise Bulloch, to whom he left his small estate -£200 2s 6d – in 1990s values some £20,000.(17) He was buried in Smithdown Road Cemetary, Toxteth, Liverpool. The long inscription on his grave concludes that he had given monumental service to the Confederate States of America, and two separate side inscriptions state that he was an ''American by Birth'' and ''Englishman by Choice.''

## The continuing struggle

The ideas that gave birth to the Confederacy did not die with the defeat of the South; they lived on and still exist to this day. Only months after the war ended Alexander H. Stephens, former vice-president of the Confederacy stated:

''Equality does not exist between blacks and whites. The one race is by nature inferior in many respects, physically and mentally, to the other. This should be received as a fixed invincible fact in all dealings with the subject. It is useless to war against the decrees of nature in attempting to make things equal which the creator has made unequal; the wise, humane, and philosophical statesman will deal with facts as he finds them.''(18)

A programme of reconstruction was embarked upon by the Federal government, but the views expressed by Stephens were commonplace, and the majority of whites in the Deep South could not accept the freed negro slaves as fellow citizens. Under these conditions a white rearguard movement developed to deny land ownership, education, and full civil rights to the freed slaves. This took its most sinister form in the anti-negro 'Klan' established in the South soon after the ending of the Civil War.

The first meeting of the Klan took place in the law office of Judge Thomas M. Jones, at Pulaski, Tennessee. The exact date is not clear, but it was probably in May or early June, 1866. All six founders were young Confederate veterans ''hungering and thirsting'' for amusement. The name was taken from the Greek word ''Kuklos'', or circle. There is general agreement that the Klan was firstly established for amusement only, but it was a 'secret society' and the potential for such a society was soon noted by hard liners who rapidly took over the organisation and converted it into a sinister grouping, the objective of which was to ''keep the negro in his place''. The reign of the White Terror organisation had begun. Dressed in white sheets, their heads covered with tall hoods, they set out at night on raids to burn negro houses, destroy their crops, and generally terrorise the black community. Soon they were lynching any 'uppity' negroes who stood up for their rights. In June 1868, the Congressional Committee on Lawlessness and Violence released statistics showing that, in the previous two years, 373 freed slaves had been killed by whites. It was believed that on top of these figures the Ku Klux Klan had killed thousands of blacks.

1877 saw the withdrawal of Federal troops from the South. The war had been over for 12 years, and in most of the states of the South the old leaders had been able to regain control of the state governments. The old South may have 'Gone with the Wind', but with the previously slave-manned plantations still in ruins and an alternative social structure not fully operational, labour problems and social unrest were rife. As in all periods of economic crisis, extremists had a field day, and the Ku Klux Klan went from strength to strength, with their hooded marauders roaming the countryside, and preserving what they saw as the Southern way of life by lynching negro activists, scaring off 'Yankee Intruders' and any other 'traitors' to their cause.

For a further period the Klan continued to grow, until it eventually became a major force in American politics. After a period of decline, in November 1915, an Atlanta man resurrected the then defunct Klan and in a ceremony outside Atlanta he, with a handful of supporters, set up and burned a cross – the symbol of the old night riders. Of even greater concern, the same year saw the release of the notorious film *Birth of a Nation* which outlined the Klan's early history. This film was crudely racist, but played to packed houses across the United States. By 1925 the Klan had a membership of four million, and in August of that year 40,000, dressed in white robes and conical hats, marched through Washington watched by 200,000 spectators. However, November 1925 saw the leader of the Klan, 'Grand Dragon' D.C. Stephenson, sentenced to life imprisonment for assault, rape and kidnapping: his victim, Miss Oberholtzer, lived just long enough to provide testimony against the Klan chief. This did nothing for the image of the Klan. Although badly bruised and with diminished support, the Klan survived this scandal, but eventually went into a deep decline. A report from Alabama on 2 June 1952 showed that for the first year in 71 years of records, no lynchings had been reported – a symptom of the Klan's decline in popularity.

It was not until 5 December 1955 that a black woman, Rosa Parks, found enough courage to enter a bus in Montgomery, Alabama, and take a seat at the front – black passengers having previously been relegated to the rear seats. When a white man entered the bus and demanded her seat, Rosa refused, the driver stopped and she was arrested. That evening other black women from Montgomery, outraged at what had happened, organised a boycott of the bus company. A local black minister, the Reverend Martin Luther King Junior, was elected to lead the campaign. The boycott continuing until 21 December 1956, when bus segregation was declared unconstitutional. The following year King established the Interracial Society to obtain total integration into American life for blacks. Even then, 1961 saw 'Freedom Riders' – testing Southern compliance with regulations for desegregation -brutally attacked in Montgomery, Alabama.

The struggle for liberty continued under the leadership of Martin Luther King, his main adversary being the notorious Governor of Alabama, George Wallace. In June 1963 Wallace took a stand, trying to stop two black students enrolling at the University of Alabama. He was swept aside by Federal troops – the first victory for the Kennedy administration in its continuing struggle with Wallace. Like Jefferson Davis a century before, Wallace then challenged the constitutionality of Federal 'interference' in the affairs of 'his' state. The next day Medgar Evers, a field worker in the National Association for the Advancement of Colored People, and the 'Martin Luther King of Mississippi' was shot. A Mississippi white,Byron Beckworth, was later tried twice for Ever's murder. Each trial ended in a hung jury.

## "I have a dream"

Two months later, in August 1963, Martin Luther King addressed the largest civil rights demonstration ever seen in America, when over 200,000 non-violent protesters – black and white – united together in Washington, appropriately at the foot of the Lincoln Memorial, and heard him make his historic speech.

"I still have a dream, it is a dream chiefly rooted in the American dream. I have a dream that one day this nation will rise up and live out the true meaning of its creed: We hold these truths to be self evident, that all men are created equal."

As the vast crowd cheered each repetition of his refrain, "I have a dream", King described a land were all would be brothers, a place were his people would be "free at last, free at last, thank God Almighty, free at last". King was now the undisputed leader of a mighty crusade. He met with President Kennedy and other influential Americans in order to advance this crucial issue, but there was still a great distance between dream and reality in America. Violence, not social justice, was still on the agenda. Before the year was out, Kennedy, a President sympathetic to the civil rights issue, was slain in Dallas – in circumstances which remain mysterious.

On 25 March 1965, Martin Luther King was on the move again, leading 25,000 people on a 54-mile march from Selma into Montgomery, capital of Alabama, affirming the right of black men and women to vote. This peaceful march was attacked from the beginning: on the way to Montgomery mounted state troops dashed into the line of demonstrators at the Edmund Pettus bridge, near Selma; and all across America people were shocked by the televised scenes of peaceful marchers being beaten and trampled.

The struggle for civil rights in America continued, but in April 1968 an assassin's bullet killed Martin Luther King; riots then broke out in Memphis and 124 other cities across the United States. More than 68,000 soldiers were needed to end the violence; at least 40 blacks and 5 whites were killed. In the midst of the rioting, on 9 April, Martin Luther King was buried at Atlanta, Georgia.

He had been strangely unconcerned about threats to his life: the day before the assassination he told people he had seen the promised land..."So I'm happy tonight. I'm not fearing any man. Mine eyes have seen the glory of the coming of the Lord."

In the 1990s, economic decline has returned to haunt the United States, and the outcome has been the return of the Klan. A Montgomery-based civil rights organisation has identified over 300 white supremacy groups active in the United States, prominent amongst these being the Klan. As they march, carrying the "Southern Cross" – the battle flag of the Confederacy, once carried by the *Florida*, *Shenandoah*, and *Alabama* – they are a grim reminder of the legacy of the Confederate rebellion.

*The Lincoln Memorial, Wahington.*
*(Tina Hollett)*

# References

*CHAPTER 1*

1. Davis, Jefferson, *The Rise and Fall of the Confederate Government*, D. Appleton & Company, New York, 1881, Vol. I, p. 6
2. *The Rebellion Record*, New York, 1861, pp. 45 – 6
3. *Tribunal of Arbitration convened at Geneva, transmitted to Congress by the President of the United States*, 24 April1872, Vol. II, p. 12
4. Scharf, J.T., *History of the Confederate States Navy*, Albany, N. York, 1894, pp. 785 – 788
5. Johnson, Allen (ed.) , *Dictionary of American Biography*, published under the auspices of the American Council of Learned Societies. Published in USA by Charles Schribner's Sons, N.Y. Published in the UK by Oxford University Press, London, 1930.
6. Scharf, Thomas J. , *History of the Confederate States Navy*, Joseph McDonough, Albany, New York, 1894, p. 786
7. *Official Records (U.S. Navy)*, Ser. 1, p. 615
8. Soley, J.R., *The Blockade and the Cruisers*, Charles Scribner's Sons, New York, 1883, pp. 34-5
9. Bulloch, James Dunwoody, *The Secret Service of the Confederate States in Europe*, Edited by Philip Van Storen Stern, Vol. II, New York, 1959, p. 51. (Quoted from original edition: New York, 1883)
10. Taylor, David Budlong, *Steam Conquers the Atlantic*, D Appleton – Century Company, New York & London, 1939, p. 299
11. *Merchants Magazine and Commercial Review*, 1861, pp. 525-6
12. Soley, p. 181
13. Jarvis, R.C. , Transactions of the Historical Society of Lancashire and Cheshire, 1959, VIII – *''The Alabama and the Law''*, pp. 182-3
14. Wardle, A.C. , *''Mersey Built Blockade Runners of the American Civil War''*, Mariners Mirror, 1942, p. 179
15. Bulloch, *Secret Service of Confederate States*, p. 57
16. Hollett, D., *Men of Iron, the story of Cammell Laird Shipbuilders 1828-1991*, Metropolitan Borough of Wirral, 1992, p. 10
17. Bulloch, *Secret Service of Confederate States*, p. 62
18. Scharf, pp. 802 – 3
19. Wardle, A.C. (compiled by), *Blockade Runners built on Merseyside and recorded at the port of Liverpool during the American Civil War*, November, 1941
20. Scharf, p. 788
21. *Arbitration Convened at Geneva*, Vol II, p. 20
22. Hill, J.D., *Sea Dogs of the Sixties*, The University of Minnesota Press, 1935, p. 93
23. *Battles and Leaders of the (American) Civil War*, ed. Published by Fairfax Press, (N. York), 1956 – reprints (Selection from the orig. 4 vol. ed. 1887-88), Vol. II, pp. 135 – 141.

**CHAPTER 2**

1. *The Liverpool Mercury*, Saturday 14 December, 1861.
2. *Ibid.,* Same paper – same page
3. Taylor, T. E., *Running the Blockade,* 2nd edition, published by John Murray, London, 1896, p. 26
4. *Ibid.*, p. 18
5. Wardle, A.C. (compiled by), *List of Blockade Runners Built on Merseyside and Registered at the Port of Liverpool during the American Civil War, 1861-1865,*Typescrip, 1941. Held at the Liverpool Record Office, (Picton Library), Ref. Hq 387.2 WAR.
6. Taylor, T.E., p. 26
7. *The Times*, 19 and 30 December 1861
8. Soley, J.R., *The Blockade and the Cruisers,* Charles Schribner's Sons, New York, 1883, p. 176
9. *Arbitration Convened at Geneva*, Vol. II, p. 20
10. Owsley, F.L., *King Cotton Diplomacy,* The University of Chicago Press, Chicago. p. 146
11. Bulloch, J.D., *Secret Service of Confederate States,* p. 152
12. *Arbitration Convened at Geneva*, Vol. II, pp. 54 – 55
13. Soley, p. 183
14. *Ibid.*, p. 184
15. Scharf, p. 791
16. *The Times*, 14 and 31 March 1862
17. *Ibid.*
18. *The Porcupine*, 10 May 1862
19. Bulloch, J.D., *Secret Service of Confederate States*, p. 228
20. *Arbitration Convened at Geneva*, Vol. I, p. 423 (Dudley to Adams, 21 June 1862 )
21. *Ibid.*, p. 424
22.*Ibid.*, p. 467 (Evidence given by Yonge)
23. *The Career of the Alabama*, published in *The Standard*, 24 June 1864
24. Bulloch, J.D., *Secret Service of Confederate States*, p. 245
25. Semmes, Raphael, *Memoirs of Service Afloat during the War between the States*, Kelly, Piet & Co., New York, and Richard Bentley & Company, London, 1869, p. 402
26. Semmes, Raphael, *Service Afloat*, p. 409
27. *Arbitration convened at Geneva*, Vol. I, p. 475 (Affidavit of John Lathom)
28. Bulloch, J.D., *Secret Service of Confederate States*, p. 264

**CHAPTER 3**

1 The Times, 23 July 1862
2. *The Standard*, 24 June 1864
3. Soley, pp. 222 – 3
4. *The Standard*, 24, June 1864
5. Scharf, p. 790
6. Hill, p. 110
7. *The Times*, 12 August 1862
8. Walpole, Spencer, *The Life of Lord John Russell*, 2nd edition, published by Longmans, Green & Company, London and New York, 1889, Vol. II, pp. 349 – 350
9. Adams, E.D. , *Great Britain and the American Civil War*, originally published in 2 volumes by Longmans, Green & Company, London, N. York etc. , 1925. Later edition quoted from, Russell & Russell, New York, 1958, Vol. II, pp. 349-350
10. Owsley, F.L., p. 437
11. *Arbitration convened at Geneva*, Vol. I, p. 423
12. *Ibid.*, p. 510
13. Hill, pp. 193 – 208
14. *The Standard*, 24 June 1864
15. Hill, pp. 193 – 208
16. Nicolay and Hays, *Life of Lincoln*, Vol. VI. Chap. 6-8, New York, 1900
17. *The Writings of Abraham Lincoln.* Constitutional Edition, Vol VI, p. 248

18. Davis, Jefferson, *Constitutionalist*, Dunbar Roland, Vol. V, pp. 409 – 411, 414 – 415. Mississipi Department of Archives and History, 1923

19. Katz, William Loren, *Eyewitness: The Negro in American History*, Pitman Publishing Corporation, New York & London, 1968, pp. 211 – 212


CHAPTER 4

1. *Arbitration convened at Geneva*, Vol. 2, p. 50
2. *Pickett Papers*, Slidell to Benjamin, No. 32, 11 January, 1863; O.R.N.., Ser. 2 Vol. III, pp. 638 – 639
3. *Ibid.*, Slidell to Benjamin, No. 28, 4 March 1863. Ser. 2, Vol. III, pp. 705 – 707
4. *Mason Papers*, Slidell to Mason, 13 April 1863, Ser. 2, Vol. III, pp. 741 – 744
5. Soley, pp. 214 – 215
6. Scharf, pp. 803 – 804
7. Soley, p. 215
8. Scharf, p. 803
9. *List of Ships Built by Laird Brothers of Birkenhead, 1829-1893.* Printed, but unpublished, held in Reference Section, Birkenhead Central Library
10. Scharf, p. 802
11. Sinclair, A., *Two years on the Alabama*, Gay & Bird, London, 1896, pp. 69 – 70
12. Semmes, *Service Afloat*, p. 541
13. *Ibid.*, p. 542
14. *The Birkenhead and Cheshire Advertiser*, 21 February 1863
15. Bulloch, J.D., *Secret Service of Confederate States*
16. Sinclair, p. 72
17. *The Standard*, 24 June 1864
18. Owsley, F.L., pp. 441 – 442
19. Scharf, p. 792
20. Semmes, Raphael, *Service Afloat*, p. 568
21. Soley, pp. 203 – 204

22. Charnwood, Lord, 1st Baron, *Abraham Lincoln (Makers of the 19th Century)*, 2nd edition, 1917
23. *Illustrated London News*, 7 February 1863


CHAPTER 5

1. Hollett, D. , *From Cumberland to Cape Horn*, Fairplay, 1984, p. 28
2. *Illustrated London News*, 29 April 1865
3. *Ibid.*, 21 February 1863
4. *The Daily Post*, 20 February 1863
5. *Arbitration Convened at Geneva*, Vol. II, p. 35
6. Wardle, A. C., *Mersey Build Blockade Runners of the American Civil War*, Mariners Mirror, March 1942, p. 180
7. *The Daily Post*, 30 March 1863
8. *The Standard*, 24 July 1864
9. Scharf, p. 803
10. Sinclair, p. 309
11. *Ibid.*, p. 149
12. *Ibid.*, pp. 321 – 322
13. *The Standard*, 24 June 1864
14. Lawler, T.B. , *Essentials of American History*, Ginn & Company, New York & London, 1902 & 1918, p. 374
15. Brookes, Noah, *Abraham Lincoln and the downfall of American slavery*, 1894 ed., published by Putnam, New York, in series – *Heroes of the Nation*, pp. 371 – 373
16. *Chronicles of America*, Longman, 1990, p. 379
17. *Arbitration Convened at Geneva*, Vol. I, p. 22


CHAPTER 6

1. *List of Ships Built by Laird Brothers of Birkenhead*, Part I, 1829 – 1943, p. 13. Printed, but unpublished, held in Reference Section, Birkenhead Central Library

2. *Arbitration Convened at Geneva*, Vol. I, pp. 367 – 368, (Adams to Russell)
3. *Ibid.* (Deposition of C.R. Yonge), pp. 371 – 372
4. *Ibid.* (Deposition of G.T. Chapman), pp. 372 – 373
5. *Ibid.* (Adams to Russell), pp. 423 – 425
6. *Liverpool Mercury*, 10 October 1863
7. *Ibid.*, 12 October 1863
8. *Laird Brothers Correspondence* (Birkenhead), Unpublished Reference material, held by Birkenhead Central Library. Ref. H 623-8
9. *Ibid.* (Assistant Secretary at the Treasury to Laird Brothers), p. 27
10. *Liverpool Mercury*, 2 November 1863
11. Scharf, p. 785
12. *Illustrated London News*, 27 October 1866


CHAPTER 7

1. McMaster, J.B., *A School History of the United States*, American Book Company, New York, Cincinnati, Chicago, 1897, pp. 397 – 402
2. Scharf, p. 792
3. Bulloch, *Secret Service of Confederate States*, p. 180
4. Hill, pp. 207 – 211
5. Sinclair, pp. 177 – 178
6. Semmes, *Service Afloat*, p. 691
7. Hollett, D. , *From Cumberland to Cape Horn*, p. 161
8. Sinclair, p. 240
9. *New Standard Encyclopaedia and World Atlas*, published by Odhams Press Limited, London, 1932, p. 1176
10. *The Encyclopaedia Americana*, (International Edition), first published in 1829. This edition published by Americana Corporation, 1977, pp. 765 – 766
11. *Liverpool Mercury*, 17 October 1863
12. *Ibid.*, 31 October 1863
13. Scharf, p. 802

14. Soley, p. 214
15. Hill, p. 209
16. *Liverpool Mercury*, 14 and 16 January 1864


CHAPTER 8

1. Hill, p. 257
2. Sinclair, p. 257 – 258
3. *Arbitration Convened at Geneva*, Vol. I. p. 634, Paris, 13 June, 1864, (Dayton to Seward)
4. Sinclair, p. 258
5. *Arbitration Convened at Geneva*, Vol. I. pp. 634 – 635, 17 June, 1864, (Dayton to Seward)
6. *Ibid.*, Vol. I pp. 634 – 635, 17 June, 1864, (Dayton to Winslow)
7. *Dictionary of American Biography*, ref. to John A. Winslow, p. 398
8. Sinclair, p. 266
9. Hill, pp. 218 – 219
10. *Ibid.*, pp. 218 – 219
11. Semmes, *Service Afloat*, p. 763
12. *Daily News*, 29 June, 1864. Letter to editor from John Lancaster on the Deerhound, Alabama and Kearsage
13. Winslow to Welles. 21 June 1864 – Official Records Series 1 – 3: 60 – 61
14. *Daily News*, 29 June 1864. Letter to the editor from John Lancaster, on the *Deerhound, Alabama,* and *Kearsage*
15. *Arbitration Convened at Geneva*, Vol. III, p. 349, (Adams to Russell)
16. *Daily News*, 21 June 1864
17. Semmes, *Service Afloat*, p. 761
18. *Ibid.*, p. 765


CHAPTER 9

1. *Arbitration Convened at Geneva*, Vol. I, pp. 370 – 371, (Consul Lawless to Earl Russell), 26 April 1864
2. *Ibid.*, 9 May 1864, (Lawless to Russell)

3. *Ibid.*, pp. 372 – 373, (Munro to Cardwell)
4. *Ibid.*, 19 August 1864, p. 374, (Adams to Russell)
5. Scharf, p. 792
6. *Arbitration Convened at Geneva*, Vol. I, pp. 383 – 384, Pernambuco, 16 October 1864, (Butler to Hand)
7. Soley, p. 189
8. Bulloch, J.D., *Secret Service of Confederate States*, p. 196
9. *Dictionary of American Biography*, pp. 397 – 398
10. *Ibid.*, p. 302
11. *Arbitration Convened at Geneva*, Vol. I, pp. 844 – 845
12. *Ibid.*, p. 742, 29 October 1864, Deposition made by Henry C. Gratton, Teneriffe
13. *Ibid.*, p. 859, 22 February 1865, (Blanchard to Darling)
14. *Melbourne Argus*, 25 February, 1865
15. Scharf, p. 811
16. Hill, p. 249


CHAPTER 10

1. *Illustrated London News*, 25 February, 1865
2. Hopcroft, G.E., *Liverpool and the Blockade Runners*, Mersey, (magazine of the Mersey Docks & Harbour Board), April 1929, p. 250
3. *Chronicles of America*, p. 391, 4 April
4. *Ibid.*, 9 April
5. Lawler, *Essentials of American History*, p. 381
6. Charnwood, Lord, *Abraham Lincoln*, WeidenField and Nicolson, p. 391
7. Wood, William, *Captains of the Civil War*, p. 388
8. Brookes, p. 447
9. *Liverpool Mercury*, 27 April 1865


CHAPTER 11

1. *The Illustrated London News*, 6 April 1865
2. *The Birkenhead and Cheshire Advertiser*, 8 April 1865
3. *Ibid.*, 22 May 1865
4. *Ibid.*, 3 June 1865
5. *Ibid.*, 10 June 1865
6. *Ibid.*, 10 June 1865
7. Jackson, E. Bridget H.(ed.), *The Jackson and Laird Families, taken from family papers*, July 1990, Unpublished typescript. Held in Reference Section, Birkenhead Central Library.
8. *The Birkenhead and Cheshire Advertiser*, 10 June 1865
9. *Ibid.*, 7 July 1865
10. *Illustrated London News*, 14 September 1872
11. *The Birkenhead News and Advertiser*, 31 October 1874
12. *Ibid.*, quoting from the *Liverpool Daily Post*
13. *Dictionary of American Biography*, p. 581
14. *Ibid.*, pp. 123 – 130
15. *Liverpool Mercury*, 7 January 1901
16. *Ibid.*, 9 January 1901
17. *Calendar of Probate*, 1901
18. Avary, M.L. (ed.), *Recollections of Alexander Stephens*, Doubleday Page & Company, New York, 1910, p.207

# Further Reading

Adams, E.D. , *Great Britain and the American Civil War*. 2 Vol. Russell & Russell, New York, 1958

Angle, Paul M. , *The Lincoln Reader*. De Capo Press, New York, 1947

Barley, T. , *Myths of the Slave Power*. Coach House Press, 1992

Basler, Roy P. , *Abraham Lincoln: His Speeches and Writing*. De Capo Press, New York, 1946

Bernath, Stuart L. , *Squall across the Atlantic – American Civil War Cases & Diplomacy*. University of California Press, Berkeley & Los Angeles, 1970

Blake, Robert, *The Conservative Party from Peel to Churchill*. Eyre & Spottiswoode, London, 1970

Bradbury, Edna & Frank, *Here comes the Alabama*. A.A. Balkema, Cape Town & Amsterdam, 1958

Bulloch, James, *The Secret Service of the Confederate States in Europe*. (1959) Edited by Philip Van Storen Stern. 2 Vol. New York. (Original edition: New York, 1883 )

Callahan, James M. , *Diplomatic History of the Southern Confederacy*. F. Unger, New York, 1964

Cameron, Gail, & Stan Cook, *Liverpool Capital of the Slave Trade*. Birkenhead Press, 1992

Catton, Bruce, *The Story of the Union Side of the Civil War*. Victor Gollancz, London, 1957

Collins, Bruce, *The Origins of the American Civil War*. Edward Arnold, 1981

Commager, Henry Steele, *Fifty Basic Civil War Documents*. D. Van Nostrand Company, London & New York

Cook, Adrian, *The Alabama Claims – American Politics & Anglo American Relations, 1865 – 1872*. Cornell University Press, 1975

Davies D. , *The problems of Slavery in Western Culture*. Oxford University Press, 1966

Davis, Jefferson, *The Rise & Fall of the Confederate Government*. D. Appleton & Company, New York, 1881

Delany, Norman C, *John McIntosh Kell of the Raider Alabama*. University of Alabama Press, 1973

Duberman, Martin, *The Antislavery Vanguard*. Princeton University Press. Princeton, New Jersey, 1965

Dudley, Thomas H. (1893) *Three Critical Periods in our Diplomatic Relations with England during the War*. (Reprinted in *Pennsylvania Magazine of History & Biography,* Vol 17 pp 34-54)

Dupay & Dupay, *The Compact History of the Civil War*. Hawthorn & Company, 1960

Eaton, Clement, *A History of the Southern Confederacy*. The McMillan Company, 1954

Everett, Susanne, *History of Slavery*. Magna Books, 1988

Fleming, Walter Lynwood, *The Sequel of Appomattox* (Chapter on the Ku Klux Movement) Yale University Press, 1919

Foner, Eric, *Politics & Ideology in the Age of the Civil War*. Oxford University Press, 1980

Franklin, John Hope, *Reconstruction after the Civil War*. The University of Chicago Press, Chicago & London, 1961

Franklin, John Hope, *From Slavery to Freedom*. New York, 1956

Grierson, Francis, *The Valley of Shadows, the coming of the Civil War in Lincoln's Midwest*. Harper & Row, New York, 1948

Haskell, Frank A, *The Battle of Gettysburg*. Eyre & Spottiswoode London, 1958

Hawkins, Hugh, *The Abolitionists*. D.C. Heath & Co, Boston, 1964

Hill, Jim Dan, *Sea Dogs of the Sixties*. The University of Minnesota Press, 1935

Hollett, D. , *Men of Iron, the story of Cammell Laird Shipbuilders 1828 – 1991*. Metropolitan Borough of Wirral, 1992

Johannsen, Robert W.(Ed.), *The Union in Crisis*. The Free Press, New York, and Collier Macmillan, London, 1965

Katz, William Loren, *Eyewitness: The Negro in American History*. Pitman Publishing Corporation, New York & London, 1968

King, Martin Luther Jnr. , *Chaos or Community*, 1967

Lawler, Thomas Bonaventure, *Essentials of American History*. Ginn & Company, New York & London, 1902 & 1918

Leech, H.J. , *The Public Letters of John Bright M.P.* , Sampson Low, Marston & Rivington, London, 1885

Longford, Lord, *Great Lives – Abraham Lincoln*. Weidenfield & Nicolson, London, 1974

Macy, Jesse, *The Anti-Slavery Crusade, a Chronicle of the Gathering Storm*. Yale University Press, 1919

McPherson, James M. , *Battle Cry of Freedom*. Oxford University Press, 1988

McPherson James M. , *The Struggle for Equality, Abolitionists and the Negro in the Civil War and Reconstruction*. Princeton University Press, New Jersey, 1964

Merli, Frank J. *Great Britain & the Confederate Navy 1864-1865* Indiana University Press, London, 1970

Nash, Howard P. Jnr, *A Naval History of the Civil War*. A.S. Barnes & Company Inc, New York, 1972

Nicolay, John G. & John Hay, *Abraham Lincoln: A History:* 10 Vol. New York, 1900.

Owsley, Frank Lawrence, *King Cotton Diplomacy*. The University of Chicago Press, Chicago.

Owsley, Frank Lawrence, Jnr, *The C.C.S. Florida*. The University of Alabama Press, Tuscaloosa & London, 1987

Parish, Peter J. , *The American Civil War*. Holmes & Meir Inc, New York, 1975

Pole, J.R. , *Abraham Lincoln*. Oxford University Press, 1964

Potter, David M. , *Lincoln & his Party in the Secession Crisis*. Yale University Press, New Haven & London, 1942

Quarles, Benjamin, *The Negro in the Civil War*. De Capo Press, New York, 1953

Ridley, Jasper, *Lord Palmerston*. Constable & Co, London, 1970

Robinson, William M. , *The Confederate Privateers*. Yale University Press, 1928

Roland, Charles P. , *The Confederacy*. The University of Chicago Press, 1960

Rozwenc, Edwin P. , *The Causes of the Civil War*. Edward Arnold, 1981

Scharf, Thomas J. , *History of the Confederate States Navy*. Joseph McDonough, Albany, New York, 1894

Semmes, Raphael, *Memoirs of Service Afloat during the War between the States*. Kelly, Piet & Co, New York, and Richard Bentley & Company, London, 1869

Sinclair, Arthur, *Two Years on the Alabama*. Gay & Bird, London, 1896

Smith, Elbert B. , *The Death of Slavery in the United States*. The University of Chicago Press, London & Chicago, 1967

Soley, James Russell, *The Blockade and the Cruisers*. Charles Scribner's Sons, New York, 1883

Stamp, Kenneth M. , *The Causes of the Civil War*. Prentice Hall, Englewood Cliffs, New Jersey, 1965

Stowe, Harriet Beecher, *Uncle Tom's Cabin*.(Reprint) J.M. Dent, London, 1979

Taylor, Claire, *British & American Abolitionists*. Edinburgh University Press, 1974

Taylor, David Budlong, *Steam Conquers the Atlantic*. D. Appleton – Century Company, New York & London, 1939

Touzeau, J. , *The Rise and Progress of Liverpool*, Liverpool, 1910

Trelease, Allen W. , *White Terror, The Ku Klux Klan – Conspiracy and Southern Reconstruction*. Secker & Warburg, London, 1992

Trevelyan, George Macaulay, *The Life of John Bright*. Constable & Company, 1913

Williams, G. , *History of the Liverpool Privateers & Letters of Marque*. Liverpool, 1897

Woodward, Llewellyn, *The Age of Reform*. Oxford University Press, 1990

Wooster, Ralph A. , *The Secession Conventions of the South*. Princeton University Press. New Jersey, 1962

# Index

# More Great Books from Avid Publications

## THETIS -THE ADMIRALTY REGRETS -
### The Disaster in Liverpool Bay
#### by C. Warren & J. Benson

The definitive minute by minute account of this terrible tragedy in 1939 when 99 souls lost their lives as HM Submarine Thetis undertook her first and only dive. With new photographs and documents as well as a new foreword by Derek Arnold, a survivors son, and a new postscript by maritime historian David Roberts. Why didn't anyone cut open the submarine? Why was there no urgency in the Admiralty's rescue system? Did the Admiralty really regret?

ISBN 0 9521020 8 0      £11.00 inc. p&p

## HMS THETIS -SECRETS AND SCANDAL
#### by David Roberts

This book uncovers some shocking hitherto unpublished details of the events and aftermath of this terrible Submarine disaster in 1939. Why did the Official Inquiry blame nobody, explaining it away as 'an unfortunate sequence of events'?

Why did the civil action on behalf of the widows fail?

Did the Admiralty cover it up? How much did Churchill know?

How were those left behind treated?

ISBN 0 9521020 0 5      £10.50 inc. p&p

## THE FORGOTTEN EMPRESS

### - The Tragedy of the Empress of Ireland
#### By David Zeni

'...dubbed 'The 'Forgotten Empress'...the second in a shocking trio of tragedies at sea...sandwiched in between the disasters of the Titanic and the Lusitania, ...it was a sudden death... that sent Liverpool into mourning...'

Liverpool Echo

ISBN 1 902964 15 2

£12.50 inc. p&p

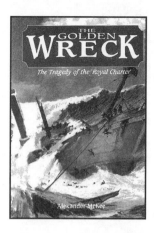

## THE GOLDEN WRECK – The Loss of the Royal Charter
By Alexander McKee

The effects great of the great hurricane of October 1859 were to shock the nation. 133 ships were sunk, 90 were badly damaged and almost 800 people lost their lives.

More than half of those that perished were on one ship - *The Royal Charter*. The worst shipwreck in Welsh history, this is the story of the *Royal Charter*…and her gold.

ISBN 1 9029640 2 0

£11.00 inc. p&p

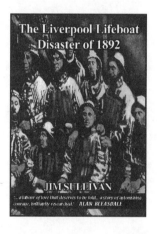

## THE LIVERPOOL LIFEBOAT DISASTER OF 1892

One man's search for a missing piece of history -
by Jim Sullivan

*'A labour of love that deserves to be told… a story of astonishing courage, brilliantly researched.'* - Alan Bleasdale

ISBN   1 902964  10  1

£8.50 inc. p& p

## LUSITANIA
by  Colin Simpson

More than eighty years on the story of the Lusitania continues to be shrouded in mystery and suspicion. What was her real cargo? Why wasn't she protected? Why did she sink so quickly?

The Facts, the fictions, but most of all…the truth.

*'A book that clamours to be read…'* - The Observer

ISBN  0 9521020  6  4

£11.00 inc. p&p

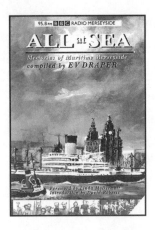

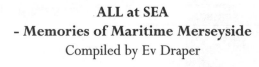

## ALL at SEA
### - Memories of Maritime Merseyside
Compiled by Ev Draper

Recollections of the men and women who sailed from and worked around the River Mersey, for trade or defence, through two World Wars to the present day.

ISBN 1 9029640 12 8
£7.25 inc. p&p

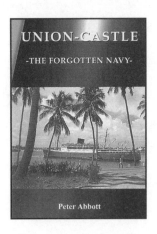

## UNION - CASTLE
### -The Forgotten Navy
by Peter Abbott

Features the Intermediate liners, The Royal East Africa Service, Round Africa vessels, coasters, general cargo ships and reefers. Also covers the Zulu War, Boer War, World War I and World War II.

ISBN 1 902964 21 7
£11.00 inc. p&p

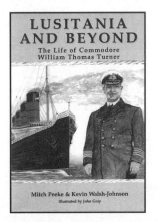

## LUSITANIA AND BEYOND
### - the Life of Captain William Thomas Turner
by Mitch Peeke and Kevin Walsh Johnson

Over the years Captain Turner has been accused of treachery, stubbornness, ignorance and much worse. This book gives the true, remarkable story of Captain William Thomas Turner, the last Master of the doomed *Lusitania*.

ISBN 1 902964
£9.50 inc. p&p

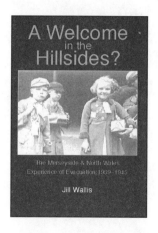

## A WELCOME IN THE HILLSIDES?
### -The Merseyside and North Wales Experience of Evacuation
### 1939 – 1945
by Jill Wallis

A book that is both informative and moving, with the real-life stories of the thousands of children who left the dangers of Merseyside for the safety of North Wales during World War II.

ISBN   1 902964 13 6

£12.00 inc. p&p

## FROM BATTLEFIELD TO BLIGHTY
### A History of Frodsham Auxiliary Hospital 1915-1919
by Arthur R Smith

The horrors of the first 'Great War' are well known, but the stories of those sent back from the 'Battlefield to Blighty' tend to be overlooked. This is the little known story in words and photographs of one of the largest auxiliary military hospitals in the country that was established at Frodsham in Cheshire during the First World War.

ISBN 1 9029640 16 0

£8.60 inc. p&p

## LIFE AT LAIRDS
### - Memories of working shipyard men
by David Roberts

*When Cammell Lairds has gone and we are a generation or two down the line who will answer the questions 'What did they do there?' 'What was it like?' This book answers the questions.*

- Sea Breezes

*A Piece of Social History* – Liverpool Echo

ISBN  0 9521020 1 3

£ 8.00 inc. p&p

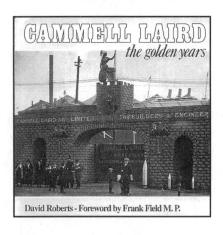

## CAMMELL LAIRD
### - the golden years
by David Roberts.

Foreword by Frank Field MP

*'Captures life in the prosperous years of the historic Birkenhead shipyard'* -
Liverpool Echo

*'Puts into perspective...the strikes...the Polaris contract...and those who
worked at the yard'* - Sea Breezes

ISBN 0 9521020 2 1

£7.50 inc. p&p

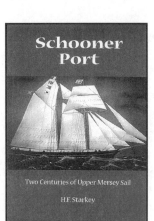

## SCHOONER PORT
### - Two Centuries of Upper Mersey Sail
by H.F. Starkey

*'Recognised as the only authoritative work on this particular subject'* - Sea
Breezes

*'Packed with hard facts and illustrated with some rare old photographs, this
rare book should command a wide readership'*.
- Liverpool Echo

ISBN 0 9521020 4 6

£10.00 inc. p&p

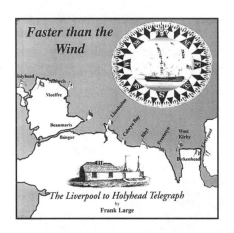

## FASTER THAN THE WIND
### - A History Guide to the Liverpool to Holyhead Telegraph.
by Frank Large

Take a journey along the one of most spectacular coastlines in
Britain, the hills and countryside of North Wales and Wirral. The
views are quite superb, and on a clear day it is possible to see just
how signals about shipping were sent along the coast to and from
Liverpool. This book contains full details of the intriguing and little
known sites of the substantial remains of the Liverpool to Holyhead
Telegraph Stations. ISBN 0 9521020 9 9 £10.00 inc. p&p

### IRON CLIPPER *'TAYLEUR'*
### – the White Star Line's 'First Titanic'
by  H.F. Starkey

'Iron Clipper' is subtitled 'The First Titanic' for it tells the story of the
first White Star liner to be lost on her maiden voyage. The *'Tayleur'*
tragedy of 1854 and the '*Titanic*' catastrophe of 1912 are disasters
which have so much in common that the many coincidences make
this book appear to be a work which is stranger than fiction.

ISBN  1 902964 00 4

£8.00 inc. p&p

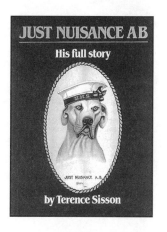

### JUST NUISANCE AB - His full story
by Terence Sisson

The amazing but true story of the only dog that was officially enlisted
into the British Royal Navy, a Great Dane whose name was Nuisance,
his official rank and name was AB Just Nuisance.

Famed for his preference for the company of navy ratings (he wasn't
too keen on Officers) in and around the famous World War II naval
base of Simonstown, South Africa, Nuisance helped many a sailor
rejoin his ship after a night on the town.

£8.00 inc. p&p

### OFF THE CUFF
– by Swasie Turner
Foreword by Alison Halford

A look at real life Police work in and around the city of Liverpool, a
book to raise your eyebrows.

*'I'd make him Chief Constable...and I should know.'*
Alison Halford
- former Asst. Chief Constable of Merseyside

ISBN 09521020  4  8

£10.50 inc. p&p

## <u>VIDEOS</u>
**CAMMELL LAIRD - Old Ships and Hardships - the story of a shipyard.**

After an extensive search for moving footage of this world famous shipyard at work a video of the history of this company has at last been compiled. The story of the yard is also told through the voices of the men who worked at Lairds; Welders, cranedrivers, electricians and plumbers, they tell of the hardships of building ships in all weathers and the lighter moments that came from some of the 'characters' of the yard.

£14.99 inc. p&p

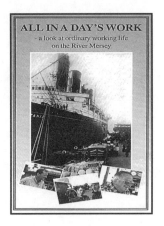

**'ALL IN A DAYS WORK' Volumes I & II
- a look at ordinary working lives on the River Mersey.**

Vessels and interviews with River Pilots, shipbuilders, shiprepairers, tugmen and dredgermen that show that the age-old crafts and seamanship itself are still as strong as they ever were on the Mersey.

Price £14.99 inc. p&p

All videos are available in international formats for £17.99 + p& p at cost.

Please state country/ format required.

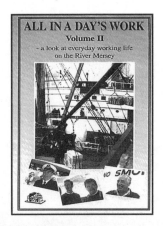

**TO ORDER BOOKS OR VIDEOS DIRECT CONTACT:-**

Avid Publications, Garth Boulevard, Hr. Bebington, Wirral, Merseyside UK. CH63 5LS.
**Tel / Fax 0151 645 2047**

Look at the books and videos via the internet on
**http://www.avidpublications.co.uk or
E-mai:l info@AvidPublications.co.uk
Note. All prices here include postage and packaging within UK.**